WADSWORTH PHILOSOPHERS SERIES

ON

LOCKE

Garrett Thomson
College of Wooster

Australia • Canada • Mexico • Singapore • Spain
United Kingdom • United States

Printed in the United States of America
1 2 3 4 5 6 7 04 03 02 01 00

For permission to use material from this text, contact us:
Web: http://www.thomsonrights.com
Fax: 1-800-730-2215
Phone: 1-800-730-2214

For more information, contact:
Wadsworth/Thomson Learning, Inc.
10 Davis Drive
Belmont, CA 94002-3098
USA
http://www.wadsworth.com

ISBN: 0-534-57628-1

CONTENTS

Introduction

Locke lived during a time of many changes. The year he was born, 1632, Galileo published his critique of the claim that the earth is the still center of the universe. Five years later, Descartes published the *Discourse on A Method*. The intellectual climate of Europe was changing. Scholastic medieval philosophy was being replaced by the new science, developed by, among others, Locke's friends, such as Newton and Boyle. This was an exciting intellectual revolution.

It was also a period of political transformation in Britain. After seven years of Civil War, England became a republic in 1649 when Locke was 17. Eleven years later England reverted to a monarchy. However, soon Protestant England was unhappy with the new Catholic kings and, in 1689, king James II, was replaced by the Protestant monarchs William and Mary. Locke was an important activist in this peaceful "revolution" which marked the end of absolute monarchy in Britain.

These political changes were intermingled with religious tensions throughout Europe. In 1648 the Thirty Years' War ended, leaving Germany destroyed. Catholic France was the major power on the continent and it was dominated by the Sun King, Louis XIV, who seemed ready to invade Protestant Netherlands. During this time of religious strife, Locke was a champion of toleration.

Locke was an active participant in the scientific, political and religious changes in the society of his time, but he was also a thinker who reflected on the meaning of these changes. He saw the need to avoid the extremes of fanatical enthusiasm on the one hand, and pessimistic scepticism, on the other. He was against authoritarianism, dogma, and the repression of individual free thought. Above all, Locke was concerned to reveal the importance of morality as a force for freedom in both politics and religion.

To achieve these goals, he argued that we need to understand what knowledge is and how we acquire it. A theory of knowledge will show us the limits of scientific inquiry. In this way, it will liberate us from scepticism and speculation and show us that our faculties are best suited for the practical concerns of moral and political thought. It will also show us the relation between reason and revelation in religion.

In brief, Locke developed a conception of political power that is not based on authority, but consent. He advanced a view of knowledge based on individual experience instead of dogma and authority.

All unmarked references are to Locke's *Essay Concerning Human Understanding*, which is divided into books, chapters and sections. The references in Chapter 10 marked 'T' are to Locke's *Two Treatises on Government*.

I would like to acknowledge my grattitude to the authors of earlier books on Locke, especially Professors Aaron, Ayers, Chappell, Dunn, Jolley and Woolhouse. I would like to thank my mother, June Thomson, who read and corrected an earlier version of this book. I dedicate this work with love to my daughter, Frances.

1

A Modest Lot

Locke's gravestone contains the following epitaph, which he composed himself:

Near this place lies John Locke. If you wonder what kind of man he was, the answer is that he was one contented with his modest lot. A scholar by training he devoted his studies wholly to the pursuit of truth....

This is a very moderate memorial for a person who might be called the founder of empiricism, whose political philosophy became enshrined in the constitution of the United States, and whose name in the eighteenth century was commonly joined with that of Newton, as the two intellectual giants of the previous century.

Locke's epitaph mirrors the mood of his life and work. Locke was born into a turbulent age, which he reacted against. In 1642, when he was 10 years old, Civil War broke out in England. Locke's father fought in the Parliamentary army against the Royalists. In 1649 king Charles I was executed and England became a republic. The violence of the time had a profound effect on Locke's outlook. His work rejects the mad passion and zeal of the Civil War and instead, it reflects a reasonable and carefully balanced attitude to life. It illustrates the virtues of serious reflection, very much in keeping with the spirit of the new generation which spurned the emotionalism of the Civil War. In this vein, Locke argues for religious toleration, for an eminently reasonable version of Christianity, and for a balanced form of government to replace the excesses of absolute monarchy.

Despite this quality of moderation, Locke had an exciting life. He was a doctor and worked with the famous scientists of the time. He was

3

active in politics and had to flee the country for fear of his life. He was a scholar, thinker and writer whose work became famous and influential during his own life-time. For the sake of convenience, we shall divide his adult life into six phases.

1) SCHOLAR IN OXFORD

Locke's father was a lawyer in Somerset, in the West of England, who worked as clerk to the Justices of Peace. Fortunately, he had good connections and, in 1647, at the age of 15, Locke gained a scholarship to the best school in the country, Westminster. This set the direction of his life. The school was connected to Christ Church College, Oxford, and in 1652 Locke won a studentship at the College. He finished his B.A. degree in 1656 and his M.A. in 1658.

Locke was not inspired by his studies of medieval Aristotelian philosophy at Oxford, and he developed several interests outside his curriculum. He studied the political and religious problems of his day, and began a collection of journals and private commonplace books which are like small encyclopedias compiled by Locke himself for his own reference purposes. It was during this period that Locke began to discover the intellectual temperament that sets him apart from other thinkers: he was a very practical person, not at all tempted to speculate but, at the same time, concerned to identify and challenge the philosophical assumptions of his age.

During this early stage of his life, Locke's main interest was medicine. He started to study it unofficially, but in earnest, in the late 1650's. At this time the emphasis on practical research and experiment was innovative and exciting. Previously, knowledge of human physiology had been based on books which formed an extension of classical Greek tradition. For Locke this new approach to medicine based on observation was a perfect antidote to the unthinking adherence to tradition reflected in this formal studies.

In 1660 Locke meet Robert Boyle, the famous chemist and founder of the Royal Society. Locke's interest widened to include natural philosophy. He read Boyle, Descartes and Gassendi. Robert Boyle, who was a wealthy aristocrat, is often called the founder of modern chemistry. He had no academic post at the University of Oxford. However, he had a laboratory in his house in the High Street, and gathered around him young scientists interested in practicing the new experimental method. Locke became an active member of this group. Boyle and Locke became close friends until Boyle's death in 1691.

While Locke was pursuing his interest in science, his academic position at Oxford became more secure. He was elected to a Senior

Studentship in 1659, to a lecturership in Greek in 1660, a Readership in Rhetoric in 1663, and a post in Moral Philosophy in 1664.

In 1661 Locke's father died. Locke's relationship with his father was especially close. He approved of the way his father had brought him up: as a young child, his father was strict, but progressively less severe as Locke grew older. By the time he was an adult, Locke was close friends with his father. Locke's father bequeathed his son a small inheritance, which made Locke's life at Oxford more comfortable and solid.

In Oxford it was considered necessary that the majority of university teachers should be clergymen. Locke was pressed to enter the church. He sought the advice of an old friend, Stratchey, who counselled him not to take orders, but to travel.

Locke later took this advice. In 1665 he was appointed as secretary for a diplomatic mission to the Elector of Brandenburg. The two-month long mission to what is now Germany failed to secure either the Elector's alliance or a promise of neutrality in the Dutch war. However, Locke enjoyed his voyage abroad.

By the time he returned to Oxford, Locke had decided that his future career would be in medicine. He refused offers for diplomatic postings in Spain and Sweden. In 1667, he met the famous physician Thomas Sydenham, who was a pioneer in the cause of medicine based on rigorous observation. Despite his decision, it was not until February 1675 that Locke received his license to practice as a medical doctor (from the University of Oxford). Although he practiced medicine intermittently, it never became his regular profession, because Locke's path in life was dramatically altered by an event in 1666.

2) LONDON WITH THE EARL OF SHAFTESBURY 1667-1675

During the summer of 1666, Locke met Lord Anthony Ashley, who was already active in politics as Chancellor of the Exchequer, and who later became the Earl of Shaftesbury and Lord Chancellor of England. Ashley was ill and came to Oxford to recuperate. He met Locke, was very impressed by him, and the two men became friends. In 1667 Locke moved to Ashley's luxurious house, Exeter House, in the Strand, in the center of London and became his secretary and physician.

Ashley was a remarkable person. Orphaned at the age of nine, he was a baronet, who apparently loved political intrigues. During the Civil War he switched from the Royalist to the Parliamentarians' side, which of course won. However, after the death of Oliver Cromwell in 1658, he was accused of plotting the return of the king (Charles II). When Charles did return, in 1660, Ashley was made a Lord and entered politics. Ashley was destined to switch sides yet again in his political life, and Locke was to become involved in these conspiracies.

Locke's move to Exeter House changed his life. He flourished. His medical studies took a leap forward in London. He became a member of the Royal Society in 1668. That year, Locke directed an operation that saved Ashley's life. He began work on a book with Sydenham, *De Arte Medica*, which was planned to review the state of medicine, but which was never finished.

More significantly, Locke became actively involved in politics. He was soon advising Ashley on the important political issues of the time and his influence spread to other politicians in Ashley's circle. He was appointed secretary of the Lords' committee on Carolina and helped draft the new constitution for the colony.

In 1667 Locke wrote an essay on toleration, which was to form the basis of his later and more famous works. In 1668, he started work on a book on economics, *Some Considerations of the Lowering of Interest and Raising the Value of Money*, which was published in 1692. In this work Locke argues for a purely economic view of interest rates, which should be set by the market rate for borrowing money rather than by law. During this period Locke formed a discussion group and, as a result of this, in 1671 Locke started work on a manuscript which was later to become the *Essay Concerning Human Understanding*.

When Ashley became the first Earl of Shaftesbury and Lord Chancellor of England in 1672, Locke was also rewarded with a new post. He became secretary in charge of the Lord Chancellor's ecclesiastical business, and later secretary to the Council of Trade and Plantations. Only a year after his appointment as Chancellor Shaftesbury had alienated the king and lost his job. However, Locke retained his post as secretary of the Council of Trade and Plantations until March 1675.

3) FRANCE 1675-1679

Towards the end of 1675 Locke left England for three and half years. The pressure of work had led to a deterioration of his bronchial problems. This prompted him to go to France where he met some of the leading scholars, philosophers and medical men. He lived in the health resort of Montpellier for over a year. He then moved to Paris for a year, where he absorbed the intellectual atmosphere of the period. He met Cartesians and anti-Cartesians, and became friendly with a pupil of the scientific philosopher Gassendi whose work was to have a strong influence on Locke.

4) POLITICS IN ENGLAND 1679-1683

6

When Locke returned to England, the country was once again in the grip of political unrest. King Charles II and his brother James were both staunch Catholics, but the majority of the people of England were Protestant. The unpopular Stuarts had managed to alienate the country and Shaftesbury had become the leader of the opposition. As a result he spent a year imprisoned in the Tower of London.

By the time Locke returned, his friend had been freed because of the pressure of the recently summoned Parliament. Shaftesbury was appointed Lord President of the Privy Council and Locke was called to work with him. Fearing that Charles' brother James would inherit the throne and impose Catholicism on the country, Parliament tried to pass a bill or law disabling this succession. As a result, the King dissolved Parliament and Shaftesbury lost his job again. Shaftesbury was soon engaged in more dangerous activities in support of the Duke of Monmouth, a natural son of Charles II and Protestant aspirant to the throne of England whom the king had banished to Holland. Shaftesbury organized clubs in support of Monmouth and tried to rouse opposition to the legitimate successor to the throne, James. It is not known how far Locke was involved in all this; he based himself in Oxford, but while there was said by a fellow college member to live "a very cunning and unintelligible life ... no one knows where he goes or when he goes or when he returns."

In July 1681, Shaftesbury was arrested on a charge of high treason and spent another few months in the Tower before being acquitted. When Monmouth himself was arrested about a year later, Shaftesbury went into hiding and escaped to Holland, where he died in 1683. Later that year Locke also fled to Holland.

5) EXILE IN HOLLAND 1683-89

Locke spent the winter of 1683-4 in Amsterdam, studying medicine and philosophy. He met the famous liberal theologian Philip van Limborch. The two men became friends and were in frequent correspondence until Locke's death.

Because of Locke's long association with Shaftesbury, the king ordered his expulsion from the studentship at Christ Church in November 1684. After Charles II's death in 1685, Monmouth mounted a rebellion to oust James II from the throne. The rebellion failed. Locke's name surfaced again as one of Monmouth's supporters and the Dutch government was asked to extradite him. For a time, Locke went into hiding under an assumed name: Dr. van den Linden. He refused a subsequent offer of a pardon from the king, saying that "having been guilty of no crime", he had "no occasion for a pardon".

7

Apart from his friendship with Limborch, Locke's stay in Holland offered two consolations. First, his health improved. Second, he had the time to write. In 1685 Locke met Leclerk, who was preparing a literary journal, called the *Bibliothèque Universelle*. Locke wrote an article explaining how he wrote and set out his commonplace books, and this article was his first published work. During this period he wrote several letters to his friend Clarke concerning education, and these were later published as *Some Thoughts Concerning Education* in 1693. In the winter of 1685 Locke wrote a long letter in Latin to Limborch regarding toleration, which was published anonymously as the *First Letter Concerning Toleration* in 1689. More importantly, Locke had been working on his *Essay Concerning Human Understanding* and, in 1688, a French abstract of the work was published in the *Bibliothèque Universelle*.

In January 1687 Locke moved to Rotterdam to become more involved in politics. After Charles II's death in 1685, his brother James II had become king. He was extremely unpopular, because he believed in absolute monarchy and seemed set to impose his Catholic religion on the country. The opposition in England was planning to install Prince William of Orange of Holland on the English throne, on the basis that he was the Protestant husband of Mary, the legitimate daughter of James II. There is little doubt that Locke moved to Rotterdam to be near and to advise Prince William, who was in The Hague. In April 1688 William decided that he would support the opposition to King James and he began to prepare his campaign to take the throne. In November 1688 he set sail for England .

6) LONDON 1689-1704

Once the Revolution had been peacefully completed, Locke returned to England in February 1689 with the Princess Mary, soon to be queen. Locke's five year exile in Holland was at an end, but he wrote to Limborch:

> I almost feel as if I were leaving my own country and my own kinsfolk...for everything that binds men together with ties stronger than the ties of blood, I have found among you in abundance.

Locke was now fifty-six years old. He was a person with a good reputation among his large circle of friends. He was soon to become a figure of national fame, because of three major publications. Soon after his return, his *Letter Concerning Toleration* was published. In 1689 his *Two Treatises on Civil Government* were also printed. In 1690 his most famous work, the *Essay Concerning Human Understanding*, also appeared.

King William offered him an ambassadorial post, but Locke preferred the humbler office of Commissioner of Appeals, which afforded him time to pursue his philosophical studies. However, Locke's weak lungs were affected by the London air, and he moved to Essex, staying with Sir Francis and Lady Masham, where he spent much of his time between 1691 and the year of his death, 1704. Lady Masham had been Locke's friend for some ten years. She and her family welcomed Locke into their home.

Despite spending much of his time outside of London, Locke was still active in politics. He was close friends with all of the important politicians of the time. In effect he was the intellectual leader of the Whig party. Locke renewed his interest in economics. He became one of the founding shareholders in the Bank of England. He and his friends formed a club for reform called the 'College', which was influential in the call for standardizing the currency to avoid the debasing of coins through clipping. In 1692, Locke published his earlier paper, *Some Considerations of the Lowering of Interest and the Raising of the Value of Money*. In 1695, he also wrote *Short Observations on a Printed Paper*, defending his economic views. In May 1696 Locke was appointed Commissioner of Trade and Plantations. He was a very active member of the new board from 1696 to 1697, attending daily meetings during the summer of 1696.

However, for the most part, Locke was dedicated to philosophical study. He published *Some Thoughts Concerning Education* in 1693. The second draft of the *Essay* appeared in 1694. His main interest was religion. The *Reasonableness of Christianity*, which was published in 1695, advocated a simpler version of Christianity, which concentrated only on the essentials of the faith. Locke was accused of being a Unitarian. In 1695 he replied to the accusations against him in a *Vindication of the Reasonableness of Christianity*. In 1696-7 Locke entered into a long debate with the Bishop of Worcester, Stillingfleet, who argued that Locke's "new way of ideas" constituted an attack on the doctrine of the Trinity. Locke wrote *A Letter to the Bishop of Worcester concerning some passages relating to Mr. Locke's Essay*. This was the first of various publications in reply to the Bishop defending the *Essay* against the claim that it is inconsistent with Christianity.

Locke had many visitors at Oates in Essex, including Isaac Newton, with whom Locke would have discussed not only science, but also Biblical criticism in which both were interested, and the scientist Molyneux, with whom Locke became close friends.

9

In the winter of 1697-8, Locke was seriously ill and, he wrote to Clarke that, for want of breath,

> I am prisoner not only to the house, but to my chair, so that never did anybody live so truly a sedentary life as I do. (25th Feb. 1698)

In 1700, he resigned his positions in London. In the last years of his life, he dedicated himself to writing a commentary on the Epistles of St. Paul, which was published posthumously in 1705.

When he died in October 1704, Locke left his personal papers to his cousin, Peter King, who later became the Lord Chancellor of England. These papers contain three thousand letters and a thousand small manuscripts, including his accounts, his notes, and journals.

In his epitaph, Locke says that he is best known through his philosophical works, the main ones of which are:

Letter on Toleration, 1689
An Essay Concerning Human Understanding, 1690
Two Treatises on Government, 1690
The Reasonableness of Christianity, 1695

What the epitaph says is perhaps true in the following sense: Locke was a modest and cautious man, who loved and sought truth "with an indifference whom it pleases or displeases." However, it is not possible to know Locke as a person through his philosophical work, because, while his academic writing is cold and unemotional, he was in fact a person with a very affectionate nature. He had deep and long lasting friendships. His private correspondence and the testimonies of his many friends reveal a surprisingly warm character, who loved children and frequently went to enormous trouble on their account. "To live," he once wrote to Esther Masham, "is to be where and with whom one likes."

2
The New Way of Ideas

The aim of the *Essay Concerning Human Understanding* is to investigate the nature of knowledge and the ability of humans to know the truth. Locke's purpose is to

> inquire into the originality, certainty and extent of human knowledge, together with the grounds and degrees of belief, opinion and assent. (I.i.2)

He is concerned with the nature and limits of knowledge partly in order to clarify the prospects of the new mechanical science of the time and to discourage needless speculation about matters beyond our capacity. Speculation encourages scepticism. Locke seeks to avoid both extremes: metaphysical speculation and impractical scepticism. Locke's primary concern, though, was to show that morality was a proper concern for our human capacities.

Locke started the *Essay,* his greatest work, in 1671, during which year he produced two drafts of the work. He wrote a third draft in 1685. The first edition of the book was published in 1690. All three early versions of the book were discovered in the Lovelace collection, which Locke bequeathed to his nephew, Peter King.

Locke conceived the *Essay* following discussions with five or six friends, probably in early 1671. One of these people was James Tyrrell and, according to his report, the discussions concerned the nature of

11

morality and religion. Perhaps the arguments reached a dead-end, because Locke suggested a new line of inquiry: the limits of human knowledge. The group asked him to prepare a paper on the topic. He set down what he himself calls

> some hasty and undigested thoughts on a subject I had never before considered (Epistle to the Reader).

Locke wrote at a time when the new science, championed by his friends Newton and Boyle, was growing in confidence. Throughout the medieval period an Aristotelian view of the universe had predominated according to which the universe was a quasi-organic piece of handiwork made by God. Changes were usually explained in terms of the inclinations of the four elements, earth, water, air and fire. The earth was portrayed as the still center of the universe.

From the early 1600s, this medieval view was being replaced by the new mechanistic and atomistic conception of the universe. This was a very dramatic change. For the first time the study of nature was based on direct observation and experiment, instead of the authority of the Bible and Aristotle. For the first time, explanations were given a mathematical form, instead of being teleological. For the first time, a wide variety of physical changes were supposed to be explained with a few causal laws. These were all new and incredibly powerful ideas, first promoted by Galileo, Descartes and Bacon. They caused fundamental changes in our view of the universe and of ourselves. They lead to the development of physics and the scientific method, advanced in Locke's time by Boyle and Newton.

Locke advocates these new ideas in the *Essay*. The work became well-known to such an extent that, together with Newton's work, it marks the demise of the Aristotelian world-view. Locke wrote the *Essay* partly to articulate the basis of the new science, and perhaps to separate it from the pseudo–science of alchemy. In so doing, he presents arguments for the new science as against the medieval world-picture.

For this reason, after applauding the greatness of Boyle, Newton, and other scientists, Locke modestly describes himself in the *Essay* as "an under–labourer clearing the ground a little and removing some of the rubbish" in the path of science. As we shall see later, part of this work is to argue against the metaphysics of Descartes (1596-1650). Descartes' work was seen as the main alternative to the scholastic tradition and Locke wants to provide a new option. He objects to Descartes' notion of innate ideas, his mind-body dualism, his conception of substance and his account of matter.

12

Locke's aim is also to show how the newly flourishing mechanical sciences of his time agree with common-sense at crucial points. The *Essay* explores the philosophical implications of the new sciences for knowledge generally. Does science really inform us of how the natural world is? In this way, the *Essay* aims to evaluate the promise of science and describe its limitations. For example, he argues that we cannot ever know the true nature of things in the world. Furthermore, we will never be able to understand the relation between material objects and the mind.

Some writers crown Locke as the founding father of empiricism. This is primarily because he stresses that all our ideas originate in experience. However, this very general claim about Locke is not strictly correct because Locke has important rationalist or non-empiricist themes running throughout his work, especially in his definition of knowledge and his view of essence. In a sense, the whole discussion of whether Locke should be called empiricist or rationalist is anachronistic. These categories did not exist at the time; they are a later invention. Nevertheless, in important ways, Locke's work is empiricist in spirit: his sustained argument to show how that all the materials of knowledge can be derived from ordinary sense experience may be viewed as an attempt to replace traditional metaphysics, both dogmatic and speculative, with what we might call today a psychological account of knowledge.

The New Way of Ideas

Locke's philosophical approach was called 'the new way of ideas'. The term 'idea' plays a central role in his whole work. To achieve his overall aims, Locke explains the nature and origin of knowledge. Simply put, his view is that knowledge is based on ideas, and hence we need to understand his conception of ideas.

Ideas are the immediate objects of perception and thought. Locke says:

> Whatsoever the mind perceive in itself or is the immediate object of perception, thought or understanding, that I call 'idea'. (I,i,8)

Ideas exist only as the objects of cognitive mental activities, such as thought and perception. They do not exist apart from such activities. Furthermore, thought and perception always must be of something and, according to Locke, this something is always an idea in the mind.

13

Whenever we perceive or think, the immediate object of perception is an idea, and the idea is essential to the identity of the thought or perception. If a person were thinking about something else, then he or she would not be having the same thought.

According to Locke, ideas are what perception is directed towards. They define the content of acts of perception. Furthermore, they cannot exist apart from the act of perceiving. In contemporary language, we should say that, according to Locke, ideas are the intentional objects of perception. As such, ideas can only have the properties that the mind perceives them to have.

According to Locke, none of the above means that we cannot perceive or think of external objects. Material objects in the external world can be the object of our perception and thought. Locke never denies that. He denies that they are the immediate objects of perception.

What is the new way of ideas? Locke's theory is that all ideas are derived from experience. He shows this, first by arguing against innate ideas, and second, by showing in detail how our ideas are derived from experience. Locke uses this explanation of the origin of ideas to give a theory of knowledge. This theory allows him to evaluate the prospects of science, to find a firm basis for morality and religion, and to reject dogma.

Against Innate Ideas

Book I of the *Essay* is an attack on the doctrine of innate ideas. At the time, this doctrine had powerful religious and political connotations: religious, because innate knowledge and ideas were assumed to be God given, and political because any appeal to innate ideas was an authoritarian argument. Innate ideas were ones that could not be argued against. Consequently, Locke's argument against innate ideas is an attempt to liberate epistemology from dogma and authority.

Locke assumes that, by showing that ideas are not innate, he will support his own positive claim that they are all derived from sensory experience. He says that at birth our minds are like "white paper, void of all characters without any ideas." (II,i,2)

He notes that one common argument in favor of innate ideas or principles is that certain principles are universally held to be true. For example, the claim that parents have an obligation to care for their children seems so obvious that anyone who understands the words will agree with it. This might be thought to be proof such principles are inherent in our understanding.

Against such an argument, Locke claims that the universal acceptance of a principle does not mean that it is innate. It must be

14

shown that the principle could not be known in any other way. Locke claims that this could not be demonstrated because there are universally accepted principles which are clearly not innate, such as 'the color white is not black.' (I,ii,18)

Furthermore, with regard to moral claims, Locke argues that there are no universally accepted principles. What is accepted may vary from group to group. Locke offers an explanation of why some principles appear innate. We are taught them when we are young and accept them without question. We forget that we learned the moral principles in this way and suppose that they are innate.

In reply, the defender of innate ideas might suggest that certain principles are in the mind at birth, but that we only come to know them at a later stage in our mental development. Locke says that this could mean two things.

- First, it could mean that we have innate capacities for learning certain truths. Locke thinks that we do have innate capacities. The denial of such capacities is not part of his philosophy. However, he points out that on these grounds, almost every true principle could be counted as innate.

- Secondly, the reply could mean that the principles lie innate in the mind. To this, Locke objects that the only evidence that a proposition is in the mind is that it is understood, and that a principle could not be innate unless it was understood at birth.

Locke thinks that innate ideas are not needed to explain knowledge. To demonstrate this, he gives a positive account of the origin of ideas – his view that all ideas are acquired from experience. This is a detailed and systematic attempt to show how a wide range of ideas can be so explained.

The Positive Program

Locke is sometimes called the founder of empiricism because of his view that the materials of knowledge are all given in experience. In Book II of the *Essay*, he claims that there are two fountains of knowledge from which all our ideas flow. These are sensation and reflection. Through sensation the mind receives simple ideas of sensible qualities (such as those of yellow, hot, cold, hard, sweet, bitter) from external objects. By reflecting on how the mind reacts to these ideas of sense, we acquire psychological ideas, such as those of perceiving and thinking.

Locke defines reflection as the "perception of the operations of our own minds within us" (II.i.4). By reflection, we acquire psychological ideas. The understanding actively performs three basic operations on the

15

simple ideas acquired through sensation: combination, comparison and abstraction. By observing its own performance of these operations, the understanding furnishes itself with ideas of its own acts, such as doubting, believing and willing.

Simple and Complex Ideas

Locke's project of showing that all ideas come from experience requires the distinction between simple and complex ideas. Simple ideas form the material for the construction of complex ones. Complex ideas are formed from simple ones, which are themselves not formed out of further ideas. He says that a simple idea is

> Uncompounded, contains in it nothing but one uniform appearance or conception in the mind, which is not distinguishable into different ideas. (II, ii,1)

Locke says that simple ideas are the smallest unit of experience; a simple idea cannot be dissected into different ideas. For this reason, he also characterizes simple ideas as those the names of which are not capable of definition. (III,iv,4). For example, red is a simple idea because it cannot be analyzed into any simpler idea and thus the word `red' cannot be defined. Locke claims that there are four kinds of simple ideas. These are:

1. Those received through one sense only, such as smell and color;

2. Those received through more than one sense, such as spatial extension, shape, and motion;

3. Those of reflection, which he sub–divides into those of thinking and volition (Locke calls the power to think, the understanding, and the power of volition, the will);

4. Those simple ideas which are received through both reflection and sensation; these include pain and pleasure, and the ideas of power, existence, unity and succession.

The essence of Locke's theory of ideas is that all simple ideas come from sensation or reflection, and that all complex ideas come from the operation of our minds on those simple ideas. This means that all ideas originate in sensation and reflection. The mind generates complex ideas from simple ones by uniting, repeating and comparing them. It can do this in an indefinite number of ways. This is how we produce ideas of monsters and of things that we have never seen.

While the mind actively constructs complex ideas, it passively receives simple ideas in experience. Locke argues that the mind is incapable of inventing new simple ideas and is restricted to those it passively receives in experience. It is just as impossible for the mind to construct or invent new simple ideas as it is for a blind person to have ideas of color.

To be able to defend systematically the claim that all ideas originate in experience, Locke classifies complex ideas according to the mental operations which compose them. When ideas are compounded, they form the idea of substances, such as gold. Also by compounding, the mind forms the ideas of modes, which may be sub-divided into simple and mixed. When simple ideas are compared, without being united, they become the idea of relations, such as being taller than. General ideas result from the mental operation of abstraction (see below). Locke's discussion of the complex ideas of substances, modes and relations is the backbone of Book II of the *Essay*.

The *Essay* is divided into four Books, as follows.
1) The first contains the arguments against innate ideas
2) The second Book is titled 'Of Ideas'. Basically its aim is to show how the complex ideas of substances, modes and relations are formed. It contains Locke's famous discussions of primary and secondary qualities, the mind-body relation, and personal identity.
3) The third Book is 'Of Words' which contains Locke's theory of language and his distinction between real and nominal essence
4) The fourth is 'Of Knowledge and Opinion' in which Locke explains his theory of knowledge.

Abstract Ideas

The simple ideas received from sensation are always of particulars. We perceive this particular shape, this specific color. Abstraction is the mental operation by which these particular simple ideas become converted into general ideas, such those of a triangle in general and of colors in general. As we shall see later, Locke's account of the formation of general and abstract ideas is important for him in defending his anti-Platonic view that only particular things exist. He says: "All things that exist are only particulars." (III,iii,6)

In Book II Locke describes the process of abstraction as one where the mind perceives a complex idea and then focuses on one aspect

17

of that idea. For example, we perceive whiteness as part of our ideas of chalk and snow. By focusing on that aspect, we acquire the general idea of whiteness. In Book III he describes the process of abstraction slightly differently, as one of leaving out the differences between a group of particulars, and retaining only what is common to them all. (III, iii,7) For example, we focus on what Peter, James, Mary and Jane have in common and thereby acquire the general idea of a human being.

General ideas are indeterminate. Locke says that the general idea of a triangle

> must be neither oblique, nor rectangle; neither equilateral, equicrural, nor scalenon; but all and none of these at once (IV, vii, 9).

This passage has confused some readers. It is often cited in discussions on Locke because Berkeley criticizes Locke's theory of abstract ideas primarily on the basis of this passage and what it seems to imply. Berkeley's criticism is that abstract ideas are impossible, because they are composed of inconsistent parts. This criticism appears to threaten Locke's whole program, because general ideas are obviously vital to human understanding. We need them to make comparisons and attribute qualities to things. If Locke could not account for them, his project would fail.

However, Locke does not mean that the general idea of a triangle is inconsistent. He does not mean that it has incompatible parts. He means that it is constructed out of ideas which are themselves inconsistent. What Locke means to say about the general idea of a triangle is that it is indeterminate. It is not the idea of a specific kind of triangle. Locke can affirm this because ideas are the immediate objects of perception. As such they can only have the properties that the mind perceives them to have. For example, imagine an ant crawling across a field. Now, did the ant have hairs on its front left leg? If you answer no, then you seem to be asserting that the ant had a hairless front leg. A better reply would be to say the picture you formed was indeterminate with regard to this aspect. Similarly, the general idea of a triangle is indeterminate, rather than contradictory.

By showing how ideas can acquire a general or abstract content, Locke explains how language and thought are possible in a world that consists only of particular things.

3

Primary and Secondary Qualities

Are material objects really colored? Locke's primary-secondary quality distinction tries to answer this, and the more general question, 'What are material objects really like?' It identifies the philosophical implications of the corpuscular theory of matter, advanced by the leading scientists of the time. Locke made the distinction between primary and secondary qualities a piece of philosophy that passed into common-sense. The distinction had been drawn earlier by Galileo and Descartes, but Locke makes it so clear that the distinction appears almost irresistible.

Locke distinguishes ideas and qualities. Ideas in the mind are the immediate objects of perception and thought. Qualities, on the other hand, belong to external objects. Some qualities, the primary ones, are an inherent aspect of any object, whereas the secondary qualities are simply the power in an object to produce certain ideas in our minds.

The New Physical Theory

According to Locke, the physical world is corpuscular. This means that all objects are composed of tiny particles, or atoms, and of nothing else. Furthermore, the properties of any object arise from the arrangement of its component atoms, from their various shapes, sizes, movements and positions. Additionally, according to Locke, all changes in a body are the result of the impact of one body on another. In other words, all causation is mechanical.

This corpuscular theory should be contrasted with, on the one hand, the traditional Aristotelian view of the universe and, on the other hand, with Descartes' conception of matter. According to the medieval Aristotelian view, which was still taught in universities during Locke's lifetime, the universe is composed of the four elements, earth, water, fire, and air. Also, according to this view, changes in the physical world can be explained in terms of purposes and the natural tendencies of these elements.

This medieval view was first challenged by the physical theory of Descartes, developed around 1630. Descartes developed the idea that all physical changes could be explained with a few causal mathematical laws. In this sense, Descartes' physics is mechanistic, and is the forerunner of the corpuscular theory advanced later by Boyle. However, Descartes identified matter with spatial extension and, as a result, his view has two implications which were unacceptable for corpuscular theorists, such as Boyle. First, Descartes' view implies that all matter is infinitely divisible, like space and, therefore, that there are no indivisible atoms. The atomists could not agree with this aspect of Descartes' position. Second, by identifying matter and extension, Descartes rules out the possibility of an empty vacuum. Descartes conceived the universe as swirling vortex of matter in which there was no empty space at all. In contrast, the atomists conceived of atoms as discrete pieces of matter separated by a vacuum.

Locke's primary-secondary quality distinction arises from the attempt to apply the corpuscular theory to perception. We should explain our perception of the ideas of secondary qualities in terms of the action of corpuscles on our sensory organs. This is because there is no other way in which the thing perceived can affect the perceiver's sense organs, except through the contact of imperceptibly small particles. Bodies must produce ideas in us through such a mechanism, because there is no other form of causation. As we would say now, our perception of colors is due to the operation of light waves on the retina; our perception of sounds is due to the wave motion of air molecules on the ear. Scientists of the Locke's time were not as knowledgeable as we are today about the specifics of the mechanisms. However, they were clear that perception could only work according to some such mechanism.

Locke argues the need for such a mechanism, but not for its sufficiency. Sense-perception is also a psychological or mental act:

20

Whatever impressions are made on the outward parts, if they
are not taken notice of within, there is no perception (II,ix,3)

Locke saw that these points show the need for a primary-secondary
quality distinction.

The Distinction

The need for a causal mechanism in perception is the basis of the
famous distinction. Locke makes the distinction in the following way.
The primary qualities of bodies are "those which are utterly inseparable
from the body in what state soever it be." (II, vii,9) These properties,
which all material things have in themselves, whether they are
perceived or not, are solidity, shape, extension, motion, and number.
No sub–division of a body can deprive it of these properties. Locke
also holds that the ideas we have of such primary qualities really
resemble the qualities themselves.

Colors, tastes, sounds, etc. are the ideas of secondary qualities.
Locke says that secondary qualities themselves are nothing in the
objects but "the power to produce the various sensations in us by their
primary qualities." (II,vii,10) The ideas of secondary qualities are
produced in us "by the operation of insensible particles on our senses."
(II,vii,13)

The distinction between primary and secondary qualities has two
parts.

a) First, primary qualities are the intrinsic properties of all material
things. In contrast, secondary qualities are merely the power of objects
to produce certain ideas in us. These secondary quality powers must
have a real basis in the object itself, and this basis is the primary
qualities of the particles which compose the object. Color in an object
is simply the arrangement of certain particles and their primary
qualities, and this is the basis of the power of that object to cause in us
the idea or sensation of color.

b) The second part of Locke's distinction is called the resemblance
thesis. The ideas of primary qualities resemble primary qualities
themselves, but the ideas of secondary qualities resemble nothing in the
object. Our ideas of colors and sounds, etc. do not resemble secondary
qualities, which are merely the powers to produce such ideas of colors
in us; nor do such ideas resemble the grounds of these powers, which
are the primary qualities of minute particles.

21

Locke's account of the distinction is more subtle and advanced than those of Descartes and Galileo. The two earlier writers tend to oppose colors as ideas in the mind with the primary qualities of objects. This fails to distinguish the idea of secondary qualities and the secondary qualities themselves. In contrast, Locke does distinguish the idea of color from the color as the quality of an object.

However, readers of Locke's text should beware because his exposition of the distinction is slightly misleading in places. First, Locke initially defines a quality as a power. This is deceptive because primary qualities are not powers; they are the intrinsic properties of things and the grounds of certain powers. On the other hand, secondary qualities are powers. Secondly, when Locke says that primary qualities are primary because they exist in objects whether these are perceived or not, this misleadingly suggests that secondary qualities might not exist in objects when they are not perceived. This is false, even on Locke's own account. Colored objects still have the power to produce certain ideas in us, even when they are not perceived.

Arguments for the Distinction

Locke gives several arguments for the two parts of the primary-secondary quality distinction. First, he argues that division of objects does not take away their primary qualities and that this shows primary qualities to be utterly inseparable from objects. In this sense, they are inherent in the object. In contrast, the minute particles of matter do not have secondary qualities. This shows that those secondary qualities are not inherent in the object. Pounding an almond will change its color and taste

Secondly, Locke draws an analogy between the ideas of secondary qualities and feelings of pain and nausea. There is nothing equivalent to the feeling of pain in the objects that cause us pain. Similarly with secondary quality ideas. There is nothing in the object itself similar to the feeling of warmth or the experience of white.

Thirdly, Locke points to perceptual illusions; a bowl of luke–warm water may feel cold to one hand and warm to another. Locke thinks that such differences of feeling can only be explained in terms of the corpuscular theory. The motion of the particles in the water and in the two hands must be different. Through the use of such examples Locke invites us to think of the physical basis of the changes in perception. For example, when the light is dimmed, we cannot see the colors of things. This does not mean that the things lose their color. The objects themselves do not change. They retain the power their causal powers, and thereby retain their color. The explanation of the phenomena is that the causal mechanism that allows us to see the colors is broken by the dimming of the light.

With such examples Locke shows that the corpuscular theory of science is sufficient to explain the causal mechanisms of perception. Furthermore, it accords with our common-sense. However, the theory gives us no reason for believing that our ideas of colors, sounds and other secondary qualities resemble qualities in objects. In this way Locke supports the resemblance thesis. Furthermore, corpuscular science explains colors and other secondary qualities in terms of the primary qualities alone. Science does not require that secondary qualities are inherent in objects. On the contrary, it explains them solely in terms of primary qualities.

According to Locke, are objects really colored? Ultimately the question hinges on what colors are. If they are ideas in our minds and nothing in the objects resembles those ideas, then external objects are not colored. Do words like 'green' stand for a certain features of private sense–experience, rather than characteristics of external objects? If Locke's answer to this question is 'yes', then it is more accurate to say that his theory implies that objects are not colored. If Locke's answer to the question is to affirm that color words pick out properties, then it would be fairer to say that his view is that objects are colored.

In one way his theory implies that objects are not colored. This is because there is nothing in the object resembling our idea of color. However, in another way, the theory does not deny that objects really are colored, because for an object to be colored is for it to have a special causal power in relation to our sensory apparatus. Locke's distinction implies that the object really does have that power. Consequently, they are colored.

Resemblance

Locke thinks that the ideas of secondary qualities, such as color, do not resemble the secondary qualities themselves. This is because these secondary qualities are merely causal powers based on the primary qualities of the particles in the object. Locke also thinks that there is a resemblance between the ideas of primary quality ideas and the primary qualities themselves. How should we understand this resemblance?

The Irish philosopher Berkeley (1685-1753) criticizes Locke's idea of resemblance. First, he complains that Locke is inconsistent because he maintains both

a)   we can only perceive our own ideas, and

b) our ideas of primary qualities resemble the qualities themselves and those of secondary qualities do not.

Berkeley argues that a) and b) are inconsistent on the grounds that resemblance requires the possibility of comparison, and that a) implies that there is no possibility of comparing ideas and qualities. In other words, b) requires what a) rules out.

Ultimately this criticism is directed against Locke's theory of perception, which we shall examine later in the chapter. Briefly, Locke would answer the criticism by arguing that he does not affirm a) above. Locke should say: 'I do not deny that we perceive external objects. On the contrary, I affirm that we do perceive them. Only I deny that we perceive them directly.'

Berkeley also argues that our ideas of primary qualities are as much subject to illusion as are those of secondary qualities. Locke points to perceptual illusions in secondary quality ideas. For example, the same water may feel hot to one hand and cold to another. Berkeley replies by pointing out that such illusions apply to primary quality ideas too. From afar things seem small; close to, they appear large. Seen from straight on, a coin may appear circular. From an angle, its shape looks elliptical. These cases seem exactly parallel to the examples of illusions in secondary quality ideas, argues Berkeley.

This criticism of Locke seems to miss the mark. Berkeley assumes that Locke's argument is the following:

1) We are prone to perceptual illusions with secondary qualities and not primary ones;
2) Consequently, in the case of primary qualities, our ideas do resemble what is the world, and in the case of secondary qualities, they do not

However, in fact, Locke is not giving this invalid argument at all. Rather his point is that such illusions are best explained using a corpuscular theory of causation, and that this theory requires that objects and particles really have primary qualities but have no properties resembling our ideas of secondary qualities.

What is the resemblance between primary qualities and the corresponding ideas? According to one interpretation of what Locke means, we must distinguish a determinate or specific quality, like a particular shape or color, from a determinable quality, like being colored or having a shape. The thesis of resemblance is about determinable qualities rather than determinate or specific qualities. The resemblance thesis is the following. With the primary qualities, things look or appear as they really are; things that look shaped really do have a shape.

But with the secondary qualities, like color, things do not appear as they are; things appear colored when really they are not.

The Theory of Perception

Locke argues for a representationalist theory of perception. According to this theory, we directly perceive ideas in our own minds. These ideas represent the objects in the external world that are the cause of the ideas. According to Locke, the fact that our ideas do represent those objects permits us to claim that we perceive external objects indirectly.

The representational theory should be contrasted with direct realism and phenomenalism. A direct realist claims that the immediate objects of perception are external objects that exist independently of our perceiving them. The phenomenalist claims that what we call external objects are simply logical constructions out of sense–data or ideas and that statements about external objects are counterfactual or hypothetical statements about how we would perceive under certain conditions.

Locke's theory of perception differs from both of these views. According to it, physical objects exist independently of our perceptions of them (thus it is distinct from phenomenalism), but those external objects are not the immediate objects of perception (thus it is distinct from direct realism).

Locke's theory looks like common-sense. However, it faces a problem, namely: how we can ever know anything about external objects when we only ever directly perceive our own ideas? In particular, how is it ever possible to know our ideas are caused by external objects and sometimes resemble them? Locke's claim that we indirectly perceive external objects depends on the statement that perceptual ideas represent those objects. Without the second, Locke cannot justifiably claim the first. How can he justify the assertion that ideas resemble objects and thereby represent them?

Locke himself recognizes these problems. He asks:

> How shall the mind, when it perceives nothing but its own ideas, know that they agree with things themselves? (IV.iv.3)

Locke responds in four ways. First, he explains how the ideas of sense do provide us with evidence for the existence and nature of external things, even though we cannot directly perceive them. Such ideas are not under the direct control of our will. Therefore, they are not produced by us. Consequently, it is reasonable to think that they are caused by external objects.

Secondly, the different senses corroborate one another. Together they testify as to the nature of external things. For example, Locke claims that qualities such as space, shape and motion are given by more than one sense, by sight and touch. Locke notes that

> The ideas we receive by sensation are often in grown people altered by the judgement without our taking notice of it (II, ix,8)

Locke gives the following example of this phenomenon. Suppose I see a globe that has a uniform color. On their own the ideas of sight would be of a "flat circle variously shadowed." However, in fact, I see the globe as a globe. This is because of the co-operation of the two senses. Sight is influenced by touch. We interpret what we see in terms of what we have touched. In other words, our sensations are affected by our perceptual judgments. This shows how the senses co-operate and, according to Locke, together the senses reveal the nature of external objects, with regard to primary qualities.

Locke tries to reinforce this point by imagining the case of a blind person who can distinguish a cube and a sphere by touch. Suppose that he regains his sight. Locke asks: Could he distinguish between the cube and sphere purely by sight, without touching them? Following Molyneux from whom he borrowed the example, Locke argues that he could not. This is because the sensations of sight and those of touch are associated by custom, and because of the custom, we can interpret the first in terms of the second.

Thirdly, Locke dismisses scepticism. It would be unreasonable to expect more evidence than that provided by our senses. For example, it is a mistake to expect a logical demonstration of the existence of external objects. Such things cannot be known with complete certainty. Furthermore, we do not need additional evidence. The senses provide all the evidence we require for the practical concerns of everyday life. Locke also gives an argument against general scepticism. No sceptic can be certain what his opinions are, and therefore no sceptic can ever disagree with Locke's claims. In this way, Locke thinks that scepticism effectively refutes itself.

Fourthly, Locke concedes that we are utterly ignorant of the way ideas are caused by external objects. He says that we cannot understand how our ideas are produced. In general, he claims that the connection between matter and mind is incomprehensible to us. As we shall see, this last point is of great importance in Locke's overall philosophy. It places a general limit on scientific knowledge which has many specific consequences.

Does Locke succeed in avoiding the apparent sceptical implications of his theory of perception? How should we evaluate these replies we find in the *Essay*? Rather than answer these questions, let us review the alternative positions. The argument for scepticism is as follows:

1. We can only ever directly perceive our own ideas
2. If we can only ever directly perceive our own ideas, then we cannot have knowledge of external objects

---

3. Therefore, we cannot have knowledge of external objects

This schema helps to classify the different views. The sceptic would argue that, since the premises are true and the argument is valid, then the conclusion is true. Direct realists, on the other hand, might claim that, because the conclusion is false and the second premise is true, then the first premise must be false. In this way the direct realist might argue that we do not perceive our own ideas but rather that we directly perceive so-called external objects.

Locke agrees with first premise of this argument and disagrees with the conclusion 3). He argues that the second premise is false. He claims that, even though we can only directly perceive our own ideas, we can still have knowledge of the external world.

4
Substance

Can all ideas be derived from experience? To show that they can, Locke divides complex ideas into three kinds: ideas of substances, modes and relations. In each case, Locke wants to demonstrate how complex ideas can be derived from simple ones by various mental processes. Whereas the mind is entirely passive with respect to simple ideas, Locke claims that the mind can actively form complex ideas from the simple ones. These activities are the mental operations of combination, abstraction and comparison. By showing how we can form complex ideas, Locke aims to justify his empiricist principles, which he will later use to evaluate the limits of knowledge.

Modes

According to Locke, modes are dependent on the existence of substances. Substances are particular things which exist by themselves. Modes are dependent on substances.

Locke sub-divides modes into the simple and the mixed. Simple modes are various combinations of the same idea. Such modes come from the operations of enlarging and combining simple ideas of the same kind. Among the simple modes Locke includes our ideas of space, time, number and infinity. For example, the idea of space is built up from repeating the extensions we meet in experience. Similarly with our ideas of numbers.

Our ideas of mixed modes originate in the combination of simple ideas of different kinds; examples of such mixed modes are triumph, murder and drunkenness. Locke's explanation of mixed modes plays an important role in his overall philosophy, which we shall explain later.

Space

Locke's conception of space can be contrasted with those of Descartes and Newton. During Locke's lifetime, Descartes' groundbreaking work in physics was beginning to wane in influence due to the publication of Newton's *Principia* in 1687. According to Descartes, matter was equivalent to spatial extension. According to this position, physics does not need the notion of impenetrability, because matter can be completely characterized in geometrical terms. It also implies that a genuine vacuum is impossible. Against this position, Locke notes that physical bodies are usually regarded as both extended and solid and that these terms are not synonymous. Furthermore, the two cannot be identified because while space offers no resistance to physical bodies, material things resist each other. Also, whereas the parts of space are inseparable, the parts of bodies can be separated (II, xiii, 14). As a consequence, matter cannot be identified with space. To reinforce this conclusion, Locke argues in favor of the possibility of a vacuum. He claims that motion ultimately requires the existence of empty space for things to move into. Furthermore, if God destroyed an object then this would create a vacuum. Consequently, matter cannot be identified with space, and thus, impenetrability is a feature of matter, in addition to extension.

Locke's rejection of Descartes does not mean that he accepts Newton's view of space. According to Newton, space is an infinite entity, like a container within which things move but which itself cannot move. Locke rejects this positive view of space. In his journals for 1678, he writes:

> Space, in itself, seems to be nothing but a capacity or
> possibility for extended bodies to be or to exist (Aaron p.156)

In other words, Locke affirms that space is not a real entity but is merely the possibility for material bodies to exist. Later in the *Essay*, Locke argues that the only alternative to this relational view of space would be to identify space with God (II,xiii,27). According to Locke, this is the only way we could possibly conceive of positive, absolute and infinite space. Locke does not endorse such an identification. However in advancing this as the only alternative to a relational theory of space, Locke is implicitly criticizing Newton's theory which posits space as an absolute infinite thing, distinct from God.

Locke's main aim in his discussion of space is to show how the idea of space can be derived from experience. He thinks that the idea of distance is given as a simple idea of sensation. The general idea of space is derived by repeating this simple idea of distance.

Number and Infinity

Locke explains how we acquire the idea of number from experience as follows: experience gives us the simple idea of a unit. Any number is simply the repetition of a unit. Of course, this explanation is restricted to whole integers and does not cover fractions.

To defend his empiricism, Locke needs to argue that the concept of infinity can be acquired through experience. He does this by arguing that infinity is only the idea of an endlessly growing progression. It is a purely quantitative concept. According to Locke, this is the only clear conception of infinity that we can have and it is an idea that can be explained in terms of sense-experience. It is the idea of a unit repeated without end.

To be clear, Locke does not think that the numerical idea of infinity is itself directly given in reflection or sensation. Rather, he thinks that it is the consequence of an operation of the mind on the simple idea of a unit that itself is given in sensation. In this way the concept of infinity is derived from experience in much the same way as that of any number.

By arguing that our only conception of the infinite is quantitative, Locke claims that the infinitude of God is beyond our comprehension. Although we think of God as infinite and we know by revelation that God is not merely a quantity, we have no positive idea of God's infinity. This is the basis of Locke's argument against the positive notion of infinity and the core of his defense of empiricism against the claim that our idea of infinity is not derived from experience. Locke's chapter on the infinite also constitutes an attack on the rationalists' conception of the infinite. For example, Spinoza argues for the existence of a single infinite and absolute substance. Against Spinoza, Locke could argue that this conception of the universe requires a positive notion of the infinite, which we do not have.

Mixed Modes

Simple modes are the consequence of the mind repeating a single idea. This is how we construct our concept of space, time, number and infinity. There are also simple modes for each of the ideas of each of the senses. For example, every spoken word is a different mode of sound.

In contrast, the ideas of mixed modes, such as 'obligation', 'drunkenness' and 'lies', are formed by combining simple ideas that are not the same (II,xxii,1). In general Locke denies the reality of mixed modes. They are

> such combinations of simple ideas as are not to be looked upon to be characteristical marks of any real beings that have a steady existence but scattered and independent ideas put together by the mind (II,xxii,1)

Modes are dependent existents that should be contrasted with substances, which have an independent existence. In the case of mixed modes, the mind combines certain ideas, which may not reflect anything real.

Substance in General

The concept of substance has had an important role in the history of philosophy. Aristotle makes the notion the cornerstone of his metaphysics by arguing that substances are the primary existents, or that other types of existing things, such as properties and relations, depend for their existence on substance. On Aristotle's conception, the endeavor to define substance becomes the attempt to determine the nature of reality itself.

Locke's discussion of the concept of substance, which takes place primarily in Chapter 23 of Book II, has been understood very differently by different interpreters of the *Essay*. For this reason, I shall outline the traditional interpretation of Locke's view and then show why many commentators today think that this is probably an incorrect reading of the text and of Locke's intentions.

Locke follows the Aristotlelian tradition in that he defines an individual substance as that which has properties and which is not itself a property of something else. He distinguishes:

1) The idea of particular substances or objects (such as the idea of the sun or of a particular rose),

2) The idea of different kinds of substances (such as the ideas of gold, lead, or oxygen) and

3) The more abstract idea of substance in general.

The Traditional Interpretation

According to the traditional reading, Locke shows how the ideas of substances in senses 1 and 2 above depend on the notion of substance in general, which he identifies as the idea of a pure substratum. According to this interpretation, Locke tries to explain why we need this concept of a pure substratum in the following three steps (II, xxiii,1).

1) Through reflection on the regularities in the ideas of sensation, we notice that certain simple ideas constantly go together, which we unite to form a complex idea. For example, the ideas of the sensible qualities of a cherry come into the mind by perception, and we notice that these qualities go together.

2) We presume that this combination of qualities must have an unknown core, or that the qualities must have a substratum in which they subsist. In this way we form our idea of a particular substance. Such an idea results from our idea of a substratum and from the combination of simple ideas which go together.

3) By abstraction from many such cases, we acquire the general notion of substratum, the idea of pure substance in general.

According to the traditional reading of Locke, the general idea of pure substance assumes that all the properties of a thing must have a support. In other words, according to Locke, since it is impossible that properties could exist by themselves, we can infer that there must be a substratum in which they subsist. Locke introduces the notion of a pure substratum to answer the question 'What is it that supports qualities and unites them into individual things?'

According to this interpretation, substance, so conceived, has no inherent nature. It is distinct from all properties because it is the support for all of an object's properties. It is the substratum which underlies all of an . object's properties. Being distinct from all properties, substance so conceived is itself property-less. It has no nature except that of supporting its inherent properties, and because it has no positive nature, it is not to be identified with any particular kind of substance. Consequently, the idea of pure substance in general conceived as a substratum must be distinguished from the ideas of particular kinds of substances, such as silver, gold or oxygen.

We can summarize Locke's reasoning to show the need for the concept of a pure substratum (according to the traditional interpretation) as follows. Take any individual object, like a cup. The cup has many properties or qualities. These qualities are universals and the cup itself is a particular and so, the cup must be distinct from each one of its properties. Being distinct from each of them, it must be distinct from all of them. However, properties cannot exist on their own; they must inhere in something. For this reason, we require the notion of a substratum in which the properties inhere and which is itself distinct from all the properties. In other words,

1. Any object is something distinct from each of its properties
2. Therefore, an object is something distinct from all its properties
3. Properties cannot exist on their own and must inhere in a substance

---

4. Thus, any object is a substance distinct from all of its properties

Any particular object consists of a pure substratum plus the properties which inhere in it. The idea that there are different kinds of substances is to be explained in terms of different sets of properties inhering in this pure substratum, which may be called 'pure substance in general'.

Problems with the Traditional Reading

This traditional way of understanding Locke presents three problems

1) Is it consistent with Locke's empiricism?

By identifying the notion of substance in general with the concept of a pure substratum, the traditional intepretation of Locke apparently makes the notion of pure substance in general an anomaly in the empiricist part of Locke's program. It is difficult to see how such a concept explained in terms of a pure sunstratum could be acquired from experience.

Locke affirms that all ideas must be derived from experience. However, it seems that we cannot derive the idea of a pure substratum from experience. Yet apparently Locke argues that we need such a concept. Logic and reason seem to require such a concept, while experience appears to deny it. On the traditional interpretation of Locke, there is clearly a conflict between Locke's empiricism and what he takes to be a demand of reason.

Locke was aware of this tension. He says that we cannot have the idea of pure substratum by sensation or reflection. He also calls the idea confused, and claims that if any idea had to be innate it would be this one (See II, 23 & 37). It appears that Locke admits that the notion of pure substance in general is inconsistent with his empiricist views on the origin of ideas. How then, does he resolve the conflict?

According to the traditional interpretation, despite his comments to the contrary, Locke really thinks that the idea of a pure substratum can be derived from experience. The mind experiences ideas of different qualities not in isolation but together in groups, and this togetherness is the basis in experience of the idea of substance.

2) Is the idea consistent with corpuscularianism?

The idea of a substratum seems to contradict the main claim of Locke's corpuscularian philosophy too, according to which all physical particulars are made of corpuscles or physical atoms and nothing more.

3) Do we really need the concept?

One problem with the earlier argument for a pure substratum is the step from premise 1. to premise 2. This step commits the fallacy of composition. Because an object is distinct from each one of its properties taken singly, we cannot conclude that it must be distinct from all of them taken together.

There may be a deeper problem with the whole argument, because it presents a two-fold choice: either an object is nothing but all of its properties, or else it is something distinct from them. The argument tries to persuade us that of these two alternatives, we should choose the latter. This dichotomy itself seems problematic. If the idea of properties without a substance is absurd, then the idea of pure substance without properties should be equally absurd.

The argument requires an illicit contrast between an object and all of its properties. If the contrast is illicit then we should not affirm that a cup is 'something' distinct from all of its properties, nor that a cup is nothing but those properties. Both alternatives hinge upon the contrast of a thing with all of its properties. Both alternatives depend on a mis-characterization of the difference between substances and properties. Every substance must be a particular type or kind of substance and, therefore, must have some properties. It is a mistake to ask the question 'Is that substance distinct from or identical to those properties?'

This question would be ill-formed if properties are neither identical to nor distinct from the substances which possess them.

Other Interpretations

Is Locke's view accurately portrayed by the traditional reading? Does Locke really accept the notion of a pure substratum? We have just seen that there are three reasons for hoping that he does not. These points give us a reason for looking for an alternative way to read the text of the *Essay*. Of course, they do not automatically mean that there is such a way.

Among the several alternative interpretations of Locke, perhaps the best known is that of Michael Ayers who argues that Locke identifies the notion of substance in general with that of real essence in general, rather than with the problematic concept of a pure substratum. Locke realizes that there are different kinds of substances in the world, such as gold and lead. Locke develops this concept in terms of the different causal powers various substances have. He says that causal powers "make a great part of our complex ideas of substances." (II.xxiii,7) In Book III of the *Essay*, Locke takes this idea further by distinguishing real and nominal essence. The real essence of a substance kind, such as gold or lead, is its structure that explains the observable features that members of that kind have in common. Gold has an underlying atomic strcture that explains its color, durability, weight etc. This is its real essence. Locke's concept of real essence will be explained more fully in the next chapter.

Ayers claims that, for Locke, the notion of substance in general is simply the notion of the determinable of which specific real essences are particular determinations, rather than being an entity distinct from all its properties. In other words, with "substance in general" Locke refers to real essence in general. According to Ayers, Locke does not accept the notion of pure substratum and the problematic argument for its introduction. In this way, Ayers' interpretation of Locke is attractive, because it apparently solves the anomalies in Locke's position mentioned earlier.

Other commentators also reject the claim that Locke supports the notion of a pure substratum, but without identifying substance with real essence in general as Ayers does. They argue that when Locke discusses the notion of pure substratum, he is simply referring to a philosophical position inherent in common speech, without endorsing it.

Locke also discusses the nature of substance in Chapter xiii of Book II, in the sections on space. This part of the *Essay* substantiates the claim that Locke did not endorse the notion of substratum. He writes sarcastically of it:

> we have no idea of what it is, but only a confused and obscure one of what it does. (II, xiii, 19)

Locke tells the story of a man who claims that the world is supported by an elephant. What supports the elephant? A tortoise. Locke says sarcastically that if the man had thought of the word 'substance' he could have dispensed with the animals.

These alternative readings of Locke make better sense of Locke's overall aims than the traditional one does. Locke's objective is to identify the notion of substance in order to point out that the concept is almost without content and is vague and confused. In this way, he can disarm any attempt to use the concept for philosophical purposes.

Understood in this way Locke's position on substance constitutes an attempt to undermine both the scholastic Aristotleian world view and the philosophy of Descartes. Descartes inherits the Aristotelian notion of substance and employs it in his proof of mind-body dualism, which Locke rejects, as we shall see later.

Relations: Causality

Locke divides complex ideas into three types. The third, which consists of our ideas of relations, arises from the mental act of comparing other ideas. Words like 'mother', and 'taller' stand for relational ideas. To support his empiricist claim regarding the origin of our ideas, Locke argues that all ideas of relations arise from our simple ideas (II, xxv,9). In particular he examines the relational ideas of cause and identity, both of which might thought to be innate or inexplicable on Locke's theory. We shall examine his theory of identity in chapter 6 and now briefly concentrate on causality.

The later British empiricist philosopher David Hume (1711-1776) argues for the sceptical conclusion that the idea of cause as a necessary connection between events cannot be derived from experience by abstraction. Hume claims that we have no sense impression of such a necessary connection, but only of one event following another. Hume claims that we do not perceive one event actually producing another, but only regularities in our simple ideas. Hume's later work underscores Locke's concern about causality. How can this idea be acquired from experience? Hume argues that it cannot.

Locke, however, does not maintain a sceptical view of causation. He defines a cause as 'that which makes any thing....begin to be' (II,26,2) and notes the importance of this concept of causality. It is "the most comprehensive relation" (II,xxv,11). Furthermore, he uses the notion in his own theories: for example, in his definition of secondary qualities as causal powers.

For these reasons, contrary to Hume's later views, Locke thinks that the concept of cause as a necessary connection between events can be derived from experience. But how? Locke suggests that the complex idea of causation is not derived from sensation alone, but rather from introspection or reflection. Through reflection, we discover that we can move our arms, or other parts of our bodies, merely by willing them to move. Locke thinks we derive the idea of active causal power from the experience of our own will, from the simple ideas of reflection. This is how we acquire the idea of one event making another happen.

Conclusion

In this chapter we have examined Locke's treatment in Book III of the *Essay* of the three types of complex ideas: the ideas of modes, of substance, and of relations. In order to defend his empiricist theory concerning ideas, Locke argues that all complex ideas are derived from simple ideas. His argument consists in case by case study of each type of concept.

However, we might question the underlying assumption of this debate between empiricism and rationalism: namely that if some of our ideas are not derived from experience, then those ideas must be innate. The debate offers only two alternatives: either ideas are innate or else acquired from experience in the ways Locke describes. There might be other alternatives. For example, concepts might be viewed as classificatory and linguistic abilities that are learnt by practice rather than mental items akin to images acquired by abstraction from experience.

In Locke's time the debate had an importance that is difficult for us today to appreciate. By arguing for his empiricist view of ideas, Locke attacks the dogmatism and authoritarianism associated at the time with the notion of innate ideas. Furthermore, by showing how all ideas are acquired from normal experience, Locke is trying to undermine traditional metaphysics that depends on ideas that cannot be acquired in this way.

5
Communication and Classification

In Book III of the *Essay* Locke claims that it is impossible to understand the nature of knowledge without first considering language, since knowledge consists of propositions (II, 33,19). Knowledge is essentially linguistic. According to Locke, "the greatest part of the questions and controversies that perplex mankind" depend on "the doubtful and uncertain use of words." (Epist:13) By becoming clear about how language works, we can learn how to avoid errors and to respect the inherent limitations of language. In these ways, the study of language is important for the overall aims of Locke's project to clarify the nature and extent of knowledge.

Part of Locke's program is to show how general words function, and in so doing, argue that traditional Aristotlelian views of classification fail. Medieval scholastic philosophers conceived the natural things grouped into fixed and eternal kinds according to a finite number of substantial forms Again this is important for Locke's overall project for the false view of classication leads to an unwarranted optimism concerning the ability of science to discover the true nature of reality.

Locke begins Book III with a general account of how language functions. In Chapters 2 to 6, he reveals the implications of this for general words and for classification. On the basis of this, in Chapter 9, he examines some of the inherent limitations in language. These he

39

distinguishes in Chapter 10 from abuses of language that arise from the careless use of it. Finally, in Chapter 11, he recommends ways to diminish the inherent imperfections of language.

Locke's work on language is not only important in relation to the overall project of the *Essay*; it is considered to be important in itself. It is one of the first attempts to give a systematic account of meaning. As such it has been influential on later analysis of linguistic meaning. Contemporary linguistic philosophy has taken up Locke's implicit point that the best way to understand concepts is by analyzing the meaning of the relevant words.

The Nature of Meaning

According to Locke, words are sounds which stand as marks for ideas in the mind of the person who uses them. Words stand directly for ideas rather than the qualities or properties of things, because the only things we know directly are our own ideas. A speaker must know directly what he or she means by the words he or she utters, and directly we only know our own ideas. A word that does not stand for an idea in the mind of the speaker would be as meaningless as a sound made by a parrot.

> Words in their primary or immediate signification stand for nothing but the ideas in the mind of him that uses them (III,ii,2)

Words stand for the ideas that give them meaning and not things in the world. Locke says it is an abuse of words to try to use them to stand for anything but our own ideas. He says that a person

> cannot make his words the signs either of qualities in things, or of the conceptions in the mind of another (III,ii,2).

This point will be important in Locke's attempt to show how language can be systematically misleading.

Locke's position requires qualification, because it may seem that he is arguing for the dubious claim that we cannot refer to things in the world, but only to our own ideas. As an antidote to this impression, we should remember that, according to Locke, ideas do represent things in the world. He calls ideas the natural signs of things. Consequently, for Locke, words stand for ideas, which in turn represent objects. Therefore, Locke's view is that words can pick out things in the world only

40

indirectly. We refer to objects through the ideas associated with a word. Locke expresses this point by saying that ideas are the primary signification of words and that things are their secondary signification.

Locke argues that the meaning of words is arbitrary. Each person can make any word stand for any idea he or she wants. However, certain words become associated with certain ideas and a connection between them is established. In this way, a word comes to stand for a specific idea and language becomes conventional. In support of this view, Locke argues that if there were a natural connection between words and things, there would be only one language (III, ii,1).

In summary, Locke makes two important claims: first, words can only stand directly for our own ideas and second, the connection between words and ideas is arbitrary. Because of these two points, we cannot assume that people mean the same thing when they utter the same word.

Language is an instrument that facilitates communication between humans who are naturally social beings. The main purpose of language is to communicate our own ideas to other people. Locke says that the ideas of other people are 'invisible' because we can only directly perceive our own ideas. By making sounds that signify or express ideas, we can communicate our thoughts to others.

Another person understands what one says when the words one utters excite in him or her ideas similar to one's own. The word 'red' stands for an idea in my mind and you understand my use of this word if it excites in you a similar idea. For this reason, it matters very much what words we use to convey our thoughts in communicating with others.

There are two important qualifications to Locke's general thesis. First, in claiming that the primary function of language is social communication, Locke does not deny that language has a private use. A person may use language to privately record his or her own thoughts. In this case, it does not matter what signs he or she uses (presumably so long as she remembers his or her code). However, because of custom, people tend to use the common language of society even for these private purposes (III, ix,3).

Second, Locke notes that there are also particle words, such as 'not', 'and', 'therefore', and 'of'. To show the importance and workings of such words, Locke analyzes the word 'but' (III,vii). He claims these words stand for logical and linguistic operations of the mind and for the subsequent connections between ideas. This point is important for Locke's advice about clarity of thought and communication.

This advice Locke derives from his general observations concerning the functioning of language. First, words can only be as clear as the ideas of the person using them. Therefore, to have clarity

41

in communication, it is necessary to have clear and distinct ideas. However, this is not sufficient. It is also necessary to use the particle and connector words correctly. Locke says that a person must connect his or her thoughts well,

> and to express well such methodical .. thoughts, he must have words to show what connection, restriction, opposition, emphasis he gives to each respective part of his discourse (III, vii,2)

For Locke, clarifying language is an important philosophical task. Unclear language is a major source of error. People are prone to use words that have a vague meaning, and to alter their sense in the course of an argument. According to Locke, we also use words when we have no idea corresponding to them. In such a case our words have no meaning and we are merely repeating sounds like a parrot. Too often, even when a person does use a word with a clear meaning, he or she does not communicate it to others.

Locke suggests various remedies for all these defects. The essence of these remedies is to have a clear idea as possible when using a word and not to change the idea in the midst of a discourse (III,xi, 26). From these suggestions, Locke develops a theory of definition, which we shall examine later.

Some Criticisms

Locke's theory of language requires that the meaning of words be explained in terms of non–verbal thoughts or ideas. For Locke, words are merely a convenient symbol or vehicle for our thoughts. Ultimately this implies that thoughts do not need language in order to have content. Thoughts can have content independently of the meaning of words. However, the relationship between thoughts and the meaning of words may be more intimate than Locke suggests, because most thoughts cannot be formed independently of language. If this is so then, contrary to Locke, any theory of the meaning of words will be at the same time an explanation of how thoughts can have content or meaning.

In this respect Locke's theory gives insufficient attention to the structural features of language. He seeks to explain the meaning of words, presumably because he takes these to be the basic units of meaning. In opposition to this, we might argue that any theory of meaning must account for the meanings of sentences, and explain how words contributes to the meaning of sentences. Sentences are not ad hoc combinations of words, because sentences have structure. Because of this structure, we are able to generate an indefinite number of sentences from a finite stock of words.

General Words

Locke says that we need general words. It is impossible for us to give a distinct name to each and every particular thing, and in any case, such names would be useless to anyone not acquainted with the particular in question. Furthermore, a language without general terms could provide no way of giving comparisons and generalisations and, therefore, would be of little use in enlarging knowledge.

According to Locke, terms become general by being the signs of general ideas and ideas become general by abstraction. As we have seen, abstraction is an activity or function of the mind by which we acquire general ideas from those particular ideas given to us in sensation and reflection. For instance, by attending selectively to the quality which a group of round things have in common and ignoring their other properties, we come to acquire the general notion of roundness. Similarly, by attending to the color that is common to chalk, snow and milk, we acquire the general concept or idea of whiteness.

This account of the meaning of general words allows Locke to suggest solutions to two old philosophical problems and to show how the relevant medieval scholastic theories are deficient. The first problem is often called the problem of universals. Some words stand for particular things. For example, names refer to particular people. However, any language must also include general words. What then do these words stand for? It might seem that general words require the existence of universal entities, such as Plato's forms. For example, it seems that the general word 'green' has meaning because it stands for a universal entity, greeness. However, many thinkers, including Locke himself, would argue against the existence of such universals. Locke says that only particular things exist. How then do general words have significance? This is the first problem, and in trying to solve it, Locke argues against scholastic theory.

The second problem is that general words function by classifiying particulars into groups. To what extent to these classifications reflect reality? Locke's answer to this question is his distinction between nominal and real essence. However, let us turn to the first problem.

The Problem of Universals

Do universals, such as greenness and justice, exist? Traditional philosophical answers to this question are often divided into two broad categories: realism and nominalism. For Locke realism and nominalism represent two extreme views; he tries to define a position intermediate between them.

Realists argue that universals do exist. Some realists, such as Plato, regard universals as real immaterial entities that exist outside space and time and are manifest in particular things. According to Plato, the universal forms are real entities. Other realists, such as Aristotle, deny that universals exist independently of particulars. They say that universals are common to all individuals of the same kind, but that such universals exist only as characteristics of particulars, and not independently of them.

At the other extreme, pure nominalists hold that there are no universals at all. General words represent nothing that really exists. The meanings of universal words have no existence independently of the mind. Thus there are no universals in the world, and there is nothing in common to any group of particulars except that they are called by the same name; in reality round things have in common only that they are called 'round'. Pure nominalism makes all classification arbitrary.

Locke tries to show that rejecting realism does not require us to go so far as accepting nominalism. His theory lies inbetween realism and nominalism. He claims that general words do have meaning, but that this does not require postulating the existence of metaphysical universal entities, such as forms. Locke claims that general words are the signs of general ideas, which are acquired by abstraction. In other words, general words, such as 'red', stand for general ideas in our minds, rather than naming universal entities such as Platonic forms. In this way, his theory is similar to nominalism.

However, Locke admits that things really do resemble one another. Locke's claims that classification has some basis in the real resemblances between things, which the mind does not invent. In this way, Locke's theory is more similar to realism than nominalism. According to Locke, the mind selectively attends to certain of these similarities and not others, and thus comes to form general concepts by abstraction. By picking out certain similarities and by abstraction, the mind forms general ideas which are capable of representing more than one individual. Therefore, for Locke, general ideas are the inventions and creatures of the understanding, and to this extent Locke's theory is anti-realist. On the other hand, these ideas have a basis in the real resemblances between things, and to this extent his theory is realist.

In summary, according to Locke, nature contains similarities: "Nature in the production of things makes several of them alike" (III,iii,13); but our general ideas are based on selctive attention: "The sorting of things is the workmanship of the understanding." (III,iii,12). In a way this makes both realism and nominalism correct. This reconciliation is based on Locke's general view of meaning: all words derive their meaning from ideas. Since, according to Locke, only particulars exist, words can only become general by standing for general ideas.

This result is also important for the overall project of the *Essay*. Locke's theory of language implies that words are the conventional signs of ideas. Therefore, to achieve clarity, it is necessary to have clear and distinct ideas. Words can only be as clear as the ideas they stand for. Locke's explanation of general words adds another dimension to this point. General words derive their meaning from general ideas which in turn depend on which similarities a person selectively attends to. Consequently, people might use the same word to stand for different systems of classification. According to Locke, it is important to recognize this and not pretend that our words stand directly for similarities in the world.

Some Criticisms

It is doubtful that Locke's solution to the ontological problem of universals can work. For, on the one hand, he says that only particulars exist, but on the other hand, he also assumes that these particulars really resemble each other. Yet resemblance itself is a universal, and so the two claims appear contradictory.

Furthermore, resemblance seems to require the existence of properties. Two things resemble each other when they are similar with respect to some property. In this way, Locke's theory also requires that properties or universals exist. His view implies a form of realism, thereby contradicting his starting point, namely that only particulars exist.

Locke simply assumes that only particulars exist. However, one might argue that universals exist too in the minimal sense that Aristotle asserts: particular things have properties which they may or may not share with other things. This should not lead us to treat such properties themselves as things; properties exist only in so far as things have them. If we accept this kind of position, then we must claim that particulars have universal properties.

Locke rejects the realist position because it suggests that for every general word, there must be some natural feature which divides things into kinds. This seems to imply that there is no indeterminacy or arbitrariness in classification, which is a claim that Locke would reject, as we shall now see.

Another Problem: Classification

Locke rejects the Platonic picture because it assumes that there are essential natures common to all things of one kind. It thus implies that for every general word, there must be some essential feature that divides natural things into fixed kinds. This means that there is no indeterminacy in classification, and that the way we classify things reflects real and essential divisions in the world. Locke rejects these claims.

We have already seen the reason for this rejection. General concepts are acquired by selectively attending to certain similarities and not to others. We form general ideas that can represent more than one particular thing by picking out certain similarities and ignoring others. Locke argues that there is some arbitrariness in our classifications because they depend on this selective attention. On the other hand, as we have also seen, Locke also claims that things really do resemble one another and that, consequently, our classifications are not entirely arbitrary. This contrast in Locke's views of classification is reflected in the way he contrasts real and nominal essence.

Real and Nominal Essence

The nominal essence of a substance type or kind, such as gold, is a complex abstract idea of something having certain characteristics. We can recognize and classify an object as a piece of gold because of its yellow color, its weight, its malleability, and so on. We associate this complex idea with the name 'gold'. The complex idea is formed by abstraction, that is by selectively attending to the secondary quality ideas that are common to the experience of this type of substance. We classify substances according to their nominal essence.

Locke contrasts the nominal essence of gold with its real essence. He defines real essence as "the being of anything whereby it is what it is" (III, 3, 15). In the case of substances, such as gold, the real essence is the internal constitution or corpuscular structure of the substance. The real essence consists of certain arrangements of the primary qualities of the minute particles of that substance type.

As such, real essence plays an important role in Locke's corpuscular theory of matter. The real essence of each substance can provide the basis for causal explanation of the observable properties of that substance type. The real essence of gold is the causal basis of its observable characteristics, which define its nominal essence. Nominal essence causally depends on real essence.

This last point is important because it reemphasizes Locke's position regarding classification. On the one hand, according to Locke, scholastic philosophers were mistaken in thinking that we classify substances according to their real essences. According to Locke, the real essence of substances is unknown. We classify in accordance with our ideas of nominal essence. The abstract idea of any nominal essence is formed by selective attention and hence has an arbitrary element. Because people may have different abstract ideas, the nominal essence of gold may differ from person to person.

On the other hand, although the nominal essences of substances are made by the mind, when the mind forms such complex ideas it is affected by underlying similarities, which are really there in nature. In other words, our classification is developed according to nominal essence, but the nominal essence of substances is founded on their real essence, which remains unknown. According to Locke, we should expect broad, though not universal, agreement in classification according to nominal essence.

In brief, the distinction between real and nominal essence allows Locke to criticize scholastic essentialist views of classification, without affirming a strong form of nominalism. In this way, the distinction shows the philosophical importance of the corpuscular hypothesis.

Definition

Locke says that a failure to distinguish between real essence and nominal essence leads to a false view of classification. Some of Locke's predecessors, the scholastic medieval philosophers, believed that all natural things have fixed eternal essences that divide them into species, and that these fixed essences can be discovered through a priori definition and reasoning alone. In contrast, Locke thinks that disputing the definitions of things is a fruitless method of inquiry since such definitions only determine the nominal essences (which are relative) and not the real essences of things. In opposing the scholastics, Locke denies that we can have a priori knowledge of the world.

To make his point even more clear, Locke gives his own positive account of the purpose and importance of definition. The function of words is to communicate our ideas. For two people to understand each other, the speaker and listener must have the same ideas. Since people may have formed a complex idea differently and still use the same word to stand for that idea, the primary purpose of definition is to make as clear as possible exactly what idea a particular word stands for. Locke warns us against abusing words by making them stand for unclear ideas or for several distinct ideas at once. Clear definitions are one remedy for this abuse.

The Prospects of Science

Locke holds that we are ignorant of the real essence of substances. He is also pessimistic concerning the possibilities of science to attain such knowledge. Yet, it may seem that contemporary science has proved Locke to be mistaken, because now we apparently have detailed knowledge of the atomic constitution of all the elements.

However, Locke's caution is based on three considerations which need to be emphasized. First, Locke has a very strict definition of knowledge according to which it requires certainty. So, even if faced by the science of today, Locke might still deny that we have knowledge of real essences.

Second, according to Locke, the observable properties of a substance depend on its real essence in much the same way that the theorems of geometry depend on its axioms. In other words, if one were to know the real essence of a substance, then one could logically deduce its observable qualities. Again, this sets a very high standard for knowledge of the real essences of substances, and as we shall see in chapter seven, Locke has an argument for claiming that we can never reach it.

Third, Locke has a general reason for thinking that even if we could have such knowledge, the distinction between nominal and real essence would not collapse. This is that the simple point that classification always depends on abstract ideas formed by selective attention.

The contrast between real and nominal essence is the basis of Locke's pessimism regarding the possibility of science yielding knowledge of nature. However, as we shall see later, it is also the basis for Locke's optimism regarding the possibility of knowledge of morality.

6
A New Understanding of the Mind

Locke's philosophy is rich in psychological implications: it contains a description of the operations of the mind, an account of the mind-body relation and a theory of personal identity. Moreover, his new way of ideas embodies a new approach to understanding the mind. First, it attempts to show how observable phenomena can be explained in terms of simple parts: complex ideas are made up of simple ideas. In this sense his view of the mind is similar his corpuscular account of matter. The first relies on simple ideas and the second on simple atoms. Secondly, Locke tries to show how all psychogical knowledge conforms in his general theory of how we acquire knowledge. Psychology does not require or provide any special modes of knowing, except what is given in experience. As we shall see, this points of departure supply a revolutionary view of the mind.

Reflection

According to Locke, we know our minds through reflection, by which he means

> that notice which the mind takes of its own operations and the manner of them by reason whereof there come to be ideas of these operations in the understanding (II,i,4)

In other words, reflection is introspection. Locke's definition shows that he has a representationalist theory of reflection: the mind does not know itself and its own operations directly, but rather mediately through ideas. In this way Locke's theory of reflection is similar to his account of perception. It implies that we do not have direct knowledge of the self or the mind, just as we do not directly perceive external objects. In reflection we only experience the ideas of mental activities such as reasoning, ·

> which ...we are apt to think these actions of some substance, which we call spirit (II,xxiii,5).

We do not have direct knowledge of the substance that supposedly constitutes the self. The mind is not an object of experience; only ideas are.

Locke postulates two basic types of mental operation: perception and volition. (II,vi,2) These form the basis of the simple ideas of reflection, because all other operations of the mind are really modifications of these two powers. For example, imagining, sense-perception, and reasoning are all forms of perception. Wishing, wanting, hoping and fearing are all modifications of volition. In addition, Locke also recognizes pleasure and pain as simple ideas of reflection. These last two play an important role in Locke's moral philosophy.

Locke has a theory of sense perception which recognizes the influence of judgment and other senses on our vision. Locke also recognizes the necessity of memory in sense perception (II,x,8). Without it we are trapped in the present instant, unable to perform other mental operations such as comparing and combining ideas. Memory for Locke is also important because it defines personal identity, as we shall soon see.

These are the basic elements that Locke requires to explain the functioning of the mind and our knowledge of it. Through these explanations, Locke tries to show how psychological knowledge conforms to the general pattern of our knowledge of the world. It does not require a special metaphysical basis any more than the other sciences do.

Freedom of the Will

In the section on power, Chapter 21 of Book II, Locke argues that freedom of the will is compatible with causal determinism. A person is free when there is nothing to prevent him or her doing what he or she wants to do. So conceived, liberty is freedom from external compulsion or obstacle, and freedom of action is compatible with actions being caused.

A typical objection to this compatibilist position is that freedom requires more than the lack of external obstacles; it requires freedom of the will. Locke argues vigorously against this objection, claiming that the notion of freedom of the will makes no sense.

First, he attacks the very idea of mental faculties such as the will. He believes that thinking of the mind as composed of faculties is equivalent to regarding it as made up of agents. He says:

> if it be reasonable to talk of faculties as distinct beings that can act ...then it is fit that we should make a speaking faculty and a dancing faculty... (II, xxi,17)

Instead of claiming that the will acts, we should affirm that the person acts. The idea of actions of the will involves the mistaken faculty theory of the mind.

Furthermore, the idea of freedom of the will involves a confusion. Freedom is nothing but a power that belongs only to agents. The will too is only an attribute or a power of an agent (II,xxi,14). Consequently, the idea of freedom of the will is a confusion.

Locke claims that freedom is a necessary condition of divine punishment and morality. Morality requires that a person must be morally responsible for his or her actions and this requires that his or her actions are free. By arguing that the notion of freedom is compatible with causality and does not require the postulation of mental faculties, Locke prepares the ground for a vision of morality that he claims to be consistent with his empiricist account of the origin of ideas.

Mind and Body

Descartes (1596-1650) claims that the mind is a substance whose essence is to be conscious or to think and which exists apart from any material body. Locke rejects the very basis of Descartes' mind-body dualism.

First, he argues that the essence of the mind is not to be conscious on the grounds that if this were so, then the mind would have

51

to be conscious all the time, which it is not. Locke argues that we are not conscious while asleep. Although he admits the possibility that we have thoughts during sleep which we forget on wakening, he claims that this is unlikely (IV, x, 9). On the contrary, Locke claims that it is more probable that we usually do not have any thoughts when we sleep dreamlessly. Given this, Locke concludes that thinking is not the essence of the mind, but only one of its operations.

Second, as we shall see, Locke rejects the idea that our personal identity consists in the identity of a non-material substance. In other words, he rejects the claim that personal identity requires the existence of a non-material mind. In this way his view differs fundamentally from Descartes'.

Third, Locke thinks that the notion of substance in general is that of something unknowable. This would apply just as much to the idea of a non-material substance as it does to material substance. If there were a non-material mind, it would be unknowable. In other words, Locke's scepticism regarding the notion of substance leads him to deny Descartes' claim that we can know that the mind is something distinct from the body. Consequently, according to Locke, there is no reason to affirm dualism and deny materialism.

In fact, Locke's official position concerning the mind–body problem is agnostic. He does not deny that there are mental substances, but neither does he deny that the mind might be a configuration of matter, or that matter thinks (IV, iii,6). Locke argues that this radical claim is a direct consequence of our inability know the causal relationship between material objects and ideas. For all we know, ideas could belong to material substances.

Furthermore, Locke claims that to deny such a possibility would be to limit the power of an omnipotent God. The claim that matter might be capable of thought is

> not much more remote from our comprehension (than) to conceive that God can, if He pleases, superadd to matter a faculty of thinking (IV, iii,6).

This passage seems to imply that, according to Locke, the idea of thinking material substance is logically possible. However, Locke also claims that matter on its own cannot give rise to thought (IV, 10,16). It requires the external influence of God.

Stillingfleet attacks Locke's failure to endorse dualism as contrary to Christian teaching. It implies the possibility that there is no immortal soul and thus might undermine morality. In reply, Locke insists that to deny the possibility that matter might think is effectively equivalent to negating the omnipotence of God. Furthermore, with impecable logic, Locke claims that we cannot prove the immortality of the soul.

In fact, Locke thinks that the existence of a non-material soul would not provide proof of personal immortality. The existence of a soul does not guarantee the continuation of consciousness. He also thinks personal immortality does not require the existence of a non-material soul substance. These claims are based on Locke's analysis of personal identity.

Personal Identity

Locke's theory of personal identity has three characteristics that make it remarkable. The first is that Locke argues for a relative theory of identity. What is it for something to be identical to something at another time? In chapter 27 of Book II, he claims that the conditions for identity vary according to the nature of the object in question. In contemporary terms, identity criteria are relative to sortal terms that indicate the kind of thing in question, such as 'horse' or 'rock'. As a consequence, the criteria for identifying the same horse will be different for identifying the same piece of rock.

Locke examines the case of compound bodies, such as a cube of sugar made up of crystals. In such a case, identity consists in the particles out of which the body is compounded. For a compound body to be identical over a period of time, all its parts should be the same over that period, although they may be differently arranged. This implies that if one atom is lost or added, the compound body will not be the same.

Locke contrasts compound bodies to living creatures. In the case of life forms, identity does not depend on their constituent particles, but instead consists in the organism partaking "of the same life." Locke explains this last idea in terms of the arrangement and organization of the particles. Organisms are not merely parcels of matter, but are a certain complex organization of parts that together determine a common life. Hence the identity of an oak is not changed because it grows. Its identity over time consists in its having the same life over that time period, which Locke explains in terms of the organization of the parts.

The Identity of Persons

The second important feature of Locke's theory of identity is that he distinguishes the concepts of a human and a person. A human being is a member of a species, whereas "a person is a thinking, intelligent being which has reason and can consider itself as itself." A person is a self-conscious, rational being. This is an important distinction because it allows for the possibility of persons who are not humans and humans who are not persons.

Furthermore, Locke claims that the criteria of identity for these two concepts differ. The conditions for the identity of a human being are similar to those of any organism, because a human being is an animal of a certain form. It is a question of the organization of the matter that composes the human body. This is what makes a human being the same over time.

In contrast, the identity of persons consists in the continuity of consciousness for it is by consciousness that our different sensations and thoughts at any time belong to the same person. The identity of persons is to be found in the identity of consciousness through time. Locke says that personal identity reaches as far back as consciousness can be extended backward to any past action or thought. He attempts to account for personal identity in terms of memory. Although Locke himself does not put it this way, self X is the same person as an earlier self Y when X's present consciousness of the past is the result of Y's consciousness in the past of what was then present. I am the same person as I was ten years ago because my present memories of ten years ago are the result of my experiences then.

The third characteristic of Locke's theory is that he explicitly rejects any attempt to base personal identity on identity of any substance:

> Nothing but consciousness can unite remote existences into
> one person; the identity of substance will not do it (II, xxvii,
> 23)

In other words, according to Locke's theory, it is irrelevant to personal identity whether we are composed entirely of matter or whether there exists a non-material soul substance. This is an important development in the philosophy of mind.

In this way Locke rejects two opposing views of personal identity. First, in denying that the concept of a person is the same as that of a human being, Locke rejects that continuity of body is a criteria for being the same person. Secondly, Locke says that the identity of persons does not consist in the continuity of a mental substance. It does not depend on the identity of soul substances even if there are such things. Suppose that the soul of Socrates were reincarnated as the present Mayor of Queenborough. Even if this were the case, the Mayor of Queenborough would not be the same person as Socrates, unless the Mayor had direct consciousness 'from the inside' of the experiences of Socrates.

Furthermore, the same soul could have two alternating and distinct sets of conscious thoughts and experiences. In such a case, we would conclude that there were two alternating persons with the same soul. Furthermore, it is possible that "two thinking substances may make one person" (II,xxvii,13). In other words, it might be possible for a person to have two souls. Locke concludes that personal identity does not depend on the continuity of an unknowable mental substance. Personal identity depends on what we know directly: consciousness.

Locke uses hypothetical puzzle cases to establish his view of identity. He employs the same method to argue that the identity of bodies is irrelevant to the identity of persons or consciousness. According to Locke, two distinct consciousnesses might inhabit the same body, one by day, the other by night. In such a case, there would be two persons with one body. Conversely, the same consciousness could act in two distinct bodies. In such a case, there would be one person with two bodies. Furthermore, the same consciousness might be passed from body to body; the consciousness and memories of a prince might enter the body of a cobbler and vice–versa.

Locke agrees that normally the same person in fact will be the same human being. However, this does not imply that the concepts are the same, nor that the respective criteria for identity are the same.

Locke claims that the concept of a person, unlike that of a human being, is a

> forensic term appropriating actions and their merit; and so only belongs to intelligent agents capable of a law and happiness and misery (II,xxvii,26)

Personal identity carries the idea of responsibility for actions or that those actions in the past were mine. If A is the same person as B, then B is responsible for the actions of A. In this way, the concept is a necessary condition of responsibility and morality.

7
The Limits of Knowledge

In his journal of 1677 Locke wrote that we live

> in a state of mediocrity, finite creatures furnished with powers
> and faculties well fitted to some purposes, but very
> disproportionate to the vast and unlimited extent of things
> (V.Chappell, ed.,1994, p. 147).

This quote captures well Locke's attitude to the original questions that motivated the *Essay*. How far can our knowledge extend? Can we have knowledge of morality? To understand Locke's answers to these questions, we need to comprehend his theory of knowledge.

Knowledge

Locke's empiricism of Book II of the *Essay* concerns the ideas or concepts that form the material of knowledge. He argues that they are derived from experience. However, Locke does not think that all knowledge comes from experience. For example, we know a priori that all numbers are either odd or even. We know this through reason, not through sense experience. Yet this knowledge still requires experience, because the materials for this knowledge, the concepts or ideas of number and odd and even, are acquired from experience. In this way Locke's empiricism is compatible with the claim that reason gives us knowledge. Locke's empiricism is directed to the formation and meaning of concepts, rather than how we know.

Locke distinguishes ideas from knowledge and belief. Knowledge and belief both require making judgments; they do not consist in just having ideas. This is because, whereas ideas themselves are neither true or false, knowing and believing require making judgments that are either true or false.

This is why in Chapter I of Book IV, Locke characterizes knowledge as the perception of certain relations of agreement and disagreement between our ideas. Knowledge requires that the mind link ideas together.

Locke lists four sorts of agreement and disagreement between ideas and these constitute different kinds of knowledge.

1. Identity and Diversity

This type of knowledge is expressed by "trifling propositions" such as "red is red" and "red is not blue," which merely require the judgment that an idea is what it is and is not another.

2. Logical Relations

This kind of knowledge is obtained by judging the logical relations between ideas. It is expressed with propositions, such as "the angles of a triangle equal 180 degrees." Locke thinks that this kind of knowledge can also be found in ethics, politics, and religion (IV,iii,18), and he considers it the most extensive kind of knowledge.

3. Coexistence

Not all of the relations between ideas are logical ones. There are also regularities in our ideas when, for example, one idea is regularly accompanied by another. This is what Locke means by the relation of coexistence between ideas. He says that our knowledge of substances or physical objects consists in the judgment that the ideas of certain qualities accompany each other or belong together. For example, according to Locke, our knowledge of gold consists in the judgment that the ideas of yellowness, weight, and certain powers always accompany each other.

Locke contends that knowledge of substances through the coexistence of ideas is very limited. This is because we do not perceive the primary qualities of the atoms on which secondary qualities and our perceptions causally depend. Moreover, says Locke, we do not understand the causal relationship between qualities and ideas.

4. Real Existence

At IV, xvii, Locke says that the fourth relation is "that of the actual real existence agreeing to any idea."

Degrees of Knowledge

These four different kinds of relations between ideas give rise to three different kinds of knowledge claims, or different degrees of knowledge, which Locke describes in Chapter II of Book IV.

Intuitive knowledge is an immediate perception of agreement between ideas, which, according to Locke, leaves no room for doubt. As an example Locke cites 'three is more than two.' Locke thinks that we have intuitive knowledge of our own existence and of certain principles, such as 'every event has a cause.'

Demonstrative knowledge is not immediate, but requires intervening ideas and steps, as in a mathematical or logical proof. Because of these intervening steps, demonstrative knowledge is less certain than intuitive knowledge.

Sensitive knowledge is even less certain than demonstrative knowledge (IV, ii,14). It is the knowledge we have of particular external objects when they are actually present to our senses (IV,iii,1). This third degree of knowledge, which Locke calls "the present testimony of the senses", is the basis for our knowledge of coexistence and the real existence of objects, the third and fourth type of knowledge mentioned above.

Locke uses the term 'knowledge' in a rather special way. According to him, for a belief to qualify as knowledge, we must be certain of it, and furthermore, we must be justified in our feeling of certainty. From this, it follows that many propositions that we might ordinarily claim to know would not count as knowledge, according to Locke. For this reason, Locke declines to count beliefs that are merely probable as knowledge. He claims: "the highest probability amounts not to certainty" (IV,iii,14). Such beliefs he calls 'opinions.'

Locke recognizes that we cannot claim certainty concerning many of the things we profess to know. Nevertheless, some of these beliefs can be affirmed as true with a high probability. Consequently, in our investigation of nature and in everyday life, it is important to distinguish between beliefs or opinions that are very probably true and those that have little probability of being true, by weighing the evidence for and against a belief. However, even highly probable beliefs should not be called knowledge.

Sensible knowledge

Locke's general characterization of knowledge as a perceiving of an agreement between ideas apparently entails that knowledge is confined to ideas. It seems to preclude the possibility of knowledge of external objects and their qualities. Consequently, it seems that Locke ought to deny empirical knowledge of the world. This seems to exclude the fourth kind of knowledge mentioned above, the agreement between our ideas and real existence.

Locke tries to solve the problem in chapters iv and xi of Book IV. First, the general characterization of knowledge as a perceiving of the relations between ideas should not be taken as a formal definition that excludes knowledge of reality. Second, as we saw in chapter three, Locke argues that we can have knowledge of the world, by claiming that our ideas can represent features of reality. He claims that there are usually qualitative differences between the experience of a real object and that of a hallucination. Furthermore, our ideas have external causes. On the basis of these points and others we mentioned in chapter three, Locke concludes that the "testimony" of the senses is sufficiently certain that it "deserves the name of knowledge" (IV,xi,3).

The Extent of Knowledge

Although Locke thinks that sensible knowledge is possible, his definition of knowledge casts a pessimistic shadow on the hope that science will enlarge our knowledge of nature. At IV,xii,9 and 10, after arguing that we can only know nominal and not real essences, he claims that the new experimental method "will reach very little general knowledge concerning the species of bodies." He does not doubt that scientific progress will be useful, but he contends that we should be content with probable belief and opinion rather than insisting on true knowledge, since "our faculties are not fitted to penetrate into the internal fabric and real essences of bodies" (IV,xii,11).

Locke tries to avoid the extremes of scepticism and speculation. He seeks to do so by understanding "the horizon between what is and is not comprehensible to us." (I,i,7). According to Locke, we are given our abilities by God. God does not endow us with innate knowledge, but with capacities which enable us to acquire knowledge. With this idea, we can be confident that we can know. Within the limits of these capacities, scepticism is misplaced. Beyond those limits, speculation is redundant. So, what are the limits?

a) Real Essence

First, Locke thinks that we should not be confident about our capacity to grasp the real essence of substances, as opposed to their nominal essences. The real essence of a substance, say gold, is the underlying structure of the substance which explains its observable properties. As we have seen, Locke thinks of these real essences in terms of the underlying structure of the substance, which should be characterized in corpuscular and mechanical terms. Although Locke thinks that we should try to understand nature in these atomic terms, he is pessimistic about our ability to give true accounts of the real essence of specific substances. In other words, he does not think that we can deductively explain the observable properties of specific substances in terms of their underlying corpuscular real essence. We refer to substances in terms of their nominal essence only; their real essence remains undiscovered. Furthermore, he is doubtful of our ability to know the real essences of things because classifications are always selected by the human mind. For these reasons, he concludes that "natural philosophy is not capable of being made a science." (IV,xii,10). In other words, physics is not a science.

This sounds strange until we remember that Locke has very stringent standards for what should count as a science, just as he has for knowledge as opposed to opinion. He thinks that a science would show us deductively why things have to be as they are. A science should be a deductive system, such as geometry. The practice of physics, or of natural philosophy as it was called then, does not fit this picture. Instead, it relies on empirical observations and predictions at the level of the nominal essence of things. Sometimes Locke calls this 'experimental knowledge.'

Although physics will not be a science, in the strict sense of the word, Locke does not think that this really matters. In particular, it is not a reason for scepticism. Our faculties are God-given and trustworthy enough to be reliable for living. Our empirical observations of things are sufficient for the practical purposes of life, even if they do not yield knowledge of the real essence of substances.

b) Mind and body

There is a second aspect of the limits of knowledge: namely, we will never know how primary quality changes in a physical body cause changes in the ideas in our minds. Also, we will never know how the mind produces changes in some material things. (IV,iii,28) Mind-body interaction is a mystery, according to Locke.

It is partly for this reason, as we have seen, that Locke also professes that we will never know whether thought requires the existence of a non-material mind, or whether thought could be the property of certain material systems, such as the brain. (IV, iii, 6).

From the point of view of studying nature, the gap between thought and object, or between idea and quality, means that we cannot explain how the primary qualities of the particles composing a body cause its sensible secondary qualities. In other words, this gap reinforces the first limitation on our knowledge. It explains Locke's claim that we cannot know how the real essence of a substance underlies secondary qualities. We cannot know the mechanism.

Locke says that we can only grasp these connections as the

> effects produced by the appointment of an infinitely wise
> agent, which perfectly surpass our comprehension. (VI iii,28)

In other words, we cannot understand these connections between primary qualities and ideas as something necessary, except by thinking of them as ordained by God.

Locke sharply contrasts the gloomy prospects for scientific knowledge with those for morality. Locke argues that moral knowledge can be demonstrated therefore can be known with certainty. He says: "Our proper employment lies in those enquiries and in that sort of knowledge, which is most suited to our capacities, and carries with it our greatest interest . . . Hence I think I conclude that morality is the proper science and business of mankind in general." (IV,xii,ll).

8
Reasonable Faith

In the last decade of his life, Locke spent more and more time thinking and writing about religion. He wrote the *Reasonableness of Christianity,* replies to objections called the *Vindications,* letters to the Bishop of Worcester and commentaries on the *Epistles,* including a introductory essay on understanding St Paul's Epistles. In these works, he affirms a revolutionary approach to religion, first expounded in the *Essay* and the *Letter on Toleration.* In these works Locke argues against the religious divisions and superstitions of his time, by outlining a rational conception of Christianity. Yet, at the same time, Locke asserts the importance of religion. For example, he argues that morality requires the existence of God. He also affirms the need for revelation and faith that go beyond the limits of reason. In short, Locke affirms both the need for a rational conception of religion and for recognizing the limits of rationality. To do this, he develops an account of religious knowledge.

Knowledge of God

According to Locke, the idea of God is acquired through experience, through sensations and reflection, like all the other ideas we have. The idea is acquired by thinking of a being that combines the most desirable qualities in their most perfect form. According to Locke, this means that we do not have a positive idea of God. God's goodness is perfect; such goodness is beyond our knowledge. Similarly for all the qualities of God, and in this way He is incomprehensible.

62

Locke thinks that we can prove the existence of God. His proof is given in the *Essay* at IV, 10, and it consists of two parts. In the first part Locke proves the existence of God using the principle that everything must have a cause. From this he argues that only something eternal does not have an external cause. Anything that has a beginning must have an external cause. He concludes that there must be a first cause that is itself eternal, otherwise nothing could be explained, even our own existence.

The second part of Locke's proof is to demonstrate the nature of this eternal cause. Locke says that I am a conscious being shows that the first cause itself must be conscious. Additionally, the order in the universe shows us that the first cause must be intelligent. Furthermore, we are moral beings and so our ultimate cause must be moral too.

Locke believes that the claims of religion go beyond what reason can prove. For example, he does not deny miracles and he does not deny faith and revelation. However, Locke also argues forcefully for the reasonableness of Christianity. In simple terms, this means that the essence of Christian teaching does not contradict reason. In summary, religion can go beyond reason but it cannot contradict it.

According to Locke, divine revelation is an important source of religious belief. The importance of revelation is that, through it, God can give us direct knowledge that transcends what we could learn through the normal operation of our faculties. And, according to Locke, we can know for certain that what God reveals to us will be true. However, what is more problematic, of course, is identifying truly divine revelations.

According to Locke, this cannot be known for certain. We cannot know for certain that there has been a divine revelation, nor what its message is. Despite this scepticism, revelation is important in religion, because through it, we do not need to have direct evidence for the content of what God reveals, but rather only for the claim that it is or has been revealed to us by Him.

Furthermore, there are signs by which we can distinguish true revelation from imagination. (IV.xix.7) Locke warns against those who think that

> Whatever groundless opinion comes to settle itself strongly upon their fancies is an illumination from the spirit of God (IV.xix.6)

For example, to avoid this error in relation to the Bible, we should look for evidential signs that the testimonies of divine revelations given in the Book are indeed from God. For instance, Locke thinks that the

63

miracle stories provide evidence that the words of Jesus are divine. Furthermore, we should check that revelations do not contradict reason. Locke says:

> When He illuminates the mind with supernatural light, He does not extinguish that which is natural.... Reason must be our last judge and guide in everything (IV,xix,14)

By 'natural light' Locke means reason. He explains that revealed knowledge cannot be gained from reason, but that it must accord with reason. In this way, religious knowledge can go beyond reason but still be reasonable.

Locke's theory of religion is primarily epistemological. It concerns how we form religious beliefs and what should count as knowledge. From this account, Locke makes judgements about how people should regulate their beliefs. For example, he claims that we should not assent to propositions for which there is not sufficient evidence. In arguing that we have a duty to avoid error, Locke distinguishes belief, faith, and knowledge. Belief is taking a proposition to be true. Knowing is seeing that it is true. As we saw in the previous chapter, Locke uses the term 'knowledge' primarily to indicate the grasping by reason of a priori truths with certainty. He also uses the term 'knowledge' for empirical knowledge that is perceived with certainty. Faith consist in beliefs supposedly derived from revelation (IV, xviii,2). As we have seen, for Locke, such beliefs will not attain the certainty required of knowledge.

However, the impossibility of certainty does not mean that we can believe or form opinions according to our wishes. We have a duty to try to believe what is true, even when we cannot attain certainty. Locke says:

> Faith is nothing but a firm assent of the mind, which if it be regulated, as is our duty, cannot be afforded to any thing but upon good reason and so cannot be opposite to it (IV, xvii,24).

Locke thinks that we have an obligation to regulate what we believe so that it accords with the truth. We must use our God-given faculties to the best of our abilities to avoid error. Failure to do this is a form of disobedience to God, because it is a misuse of His gift.

Reasonable Toleration

Locke was writing at a time when there was a proliferation of different Christian sects in Europe. Lutherans, Calvinists, Anglicans and Catholics were persecuting each other in different countries.

In opposition to this climate of intolerance, Locke advocates religious freedom. Mainly he does so on the grounds that the essence of religion is the personal relationship between the individual and God. Such a relationship cannot be regulated institutionally or politically. However, Locke also stresses the political importance of religious tolerance as something necessary for national unity and strength.

Locke's advocacy of religious tolerance goes hand in hand with his radical attempt to redefine Christianity. He tries to define the essence of Christianity in terms that seek what Christian sects would have in common. At a time when the apparent certainties of the medieval tradition were collapsing and when even the relatively new Protestant sects were squabbling, Locke was one of the few thinkers who saw these differences as unimportant compared to the simple essence of Christianity.

In the face of religious fragmentation, Locke saw his definition of the Christian faith as the only way to defend Christianity as a body of truth. When sects make contradictory claims about doctrinal matters, they cannot all be right. A possible diagnosis of such a situation is that people are making claims that go beyond what they can know. In this way, religious controversy becomes an epistemological issue. The questions of the *Essay*, such as 'what are the limits of human understanding?', become socially relevant. Sects arise because people make speculative claims that have no rational support. Religious division arises because such speculation becomes dogma. In other words, by being careful in our judgements about what we know and believe, we will become more clear about what faith requires and what it does not. This clarity will help us to not cling to uncertainties. It will help us to separate dogma and faith. This will promote religious tolerance, which in turn promotes peace and prosperity.

A Plea for Toleration

Let us look at two points: first, tolerance and second, what faith requires. Locke gives three general arguments in favor of religious tolerance.

First, churches have no right to punish and persecute because they have no political power. In this sense, a church is not like the state. States are formed when individuals give up the power or right to enforce morality on others, which they entrust to a government. This is why the state does have the power to punish people and execute laws. Churches, on the other hand, are voluntary associations, and are not based on people giving up political power. Therefore, they have no right to prosecute or persecute.

Furthermore, people entrust their property and safety to the state and the magistrates. This is part of the social contract that forms civil society. However, they do not entrust their soul to the civil authorities. This is not part of the social contract. Consequently, the church cannot work to persecute people for religious reasons through the civil authorities. In other words, the state and church have different functions. Churches have no political power because they are associations that people can join or leave freely.

Locke's second argument is based on uncertainty about religious matters. It is unlikely that any church or any individual person has the whole truth concerning theology. Given that they do not, then religious sects should be tolerant to each other. In this way Locke's attempt to define the simple essence of Christianity, which we shall examine below, supports his views on tolerance.

Third, while force and persecution might bring outward conformity, they do not bring inward conviction. Thus, they generate false religion and hypocrisy. People cannot be saved by endorsing religious creeds that they do not really believe. Therefore, religious persecution does not bring about the changes it allegedly seeks.

Locke argues for religious freedom but within limits; in particular, a religion should not do harm to individuals nor to the state. Those that do should not be tolerated. For example, the modern state should not tolerate a religion that involves human sacrifice. On this basis, Locke argues that society should not tolerate atheism. As we shall see in the next chapter, according to Locke, the existence of God is the basis of morality. Consequently he claims that atheism is detrimental to society. It undermines morality and hence social cohesion. On a similar basis, Locke rules out tolerance for religions that require allegiance to a foreign power. Such religions endanger the state. In such cases, although the state can rightly suppress a religion, it cannot do so on religious grounds. It only has that right the sake of political security. So, even in such cases, for Locke, persecution for the sake of religion should be forbidden.

At the time when Locke was writing, his views were very radical. They appear so much less today, partly because Locke's insistence on the separation of the functions of state and church and his views on toleration have become largely accepted by our society. To some extent, they have become part of common-sense.

Reasonable and Simple

State and church have different functions. For Locke, this means that we should rethink what Christianity is. There is a difference between the doctrines that are required according to the clergy of a particular church, and those that are required by the Bible. On the one hand, the requirements of churches often change with politics. On the other, those of the Bible are minimal and stay the same whatever the political climate. According to Locke, the Christianity of the Bible makes two essential demands: first, to believe that Christ is the Messiah, sent by God, and second, to live according to Christian morality. Anyone who complies with these two demands is a Christian. For Locke, Christianity ought to be a simple and reasonable faith, in stark contrast to the many creeds and dogmas of different Christian sects. In part this simplicity is why Locke calls Christianity 'reasonable'. He also means that the knowledge revealed to us by God does not contradict reason, even if it goes beyond it. Morality as revealed in the Old and New Testaments accords with the law of morality that is grasped by reason. Furthermore, reason teaches us that God is supreme and merciful. In these ways, Christianity is very reasonable.

For the period in which he was writing Locke's theory is a very radical way of understanding Christianity. For example, although Locke does not deny the Trinity, it is not listed among the minimal doctrines of a reasonable Christianity. Partly for this reason, Locke was accused of being a Unitarian by Edwards. Although he was friends with the Unitarian leader, Thomas Firmin, Locke denied being a Unitarian in the *Vinidcations,* the work which is a reply to Edwards.

Locke was obviously a believing Christian. However, he adopted a critical and historical approach to interpreting the Bible, both in his work the *Reasonableness of Christianity* and in his commentaries on the Epistles of St. Paul, to which he dedicated the last years of his life. According to Locke, the Bible has important role to play in our understanding of morality.

9
Morality:
The Business of Mankind

Towards the end of the *Essay* Locke writes:

> I think I may conclude that morality is the proper science and
> business of mankind in general (IV,xii,11)

Locke conceived the idea of writing the *Essay Concerning Human
Understanding* after discussing "the principles of morality and revealed
religion" with friends. These prompted Locke to investigate the nature
of knowledge and our ability to know the truth. However, Locke was
concerned primarily with knowledge in general because he wanted to
show how moral knowledge is possible. Locke probably hoped to show
how morality can be demonstrated as a science. There are indications in
his papers that he planned a systematic work on ethics (Aaron, p.256
fn.).

Locke is certain that moral knowledge is possible because he sees
deep similarities between mathematics and ethics. In mathematics
certainty is possible because it deals with the necessary connections
between abstract ideas whose definitions we know. Mathematics should
be contrasted with the natural sciences, where certainty is not possible
because natural objects have a real essence distinct from their nominal
essence.

According to Locke, ethics is comparable to mathematics in three
ways. First, morality concerns the necessary connections between
abstract ideas, and in this way it is like mathematics. Second, both
morals and mathematics deal with abstract objects, which are really
modes. In both cases, there is no difference between real and nominal
essence, and therefore, no possibility of ignorance on these grounds. In

this way mathematics and morality stand in stark contrast to the natural sciences in which real and nominal essence differ, Third, both morality and mathematics are prior to experience in the sense that in both we can gain knowledge by deduction or intuition without appeal to sense-experience. We can know a priori that murder is wrong, without knowing whether a murder has been committed. For this reason Locke writes:

> Moral principles require reasoning and discourse and some exercise of the mind to discover the certainty of their truth. (I,iii,4)

Because of these similarities, Locke is convinced that morality can be made into a deductive science.

Locke also points out some differences between mathematics and morals. Moral concepts are more complex than those of mathematics. Furthermore, people quarrel about moral arguments and not mathematical ones, because the former awaken personal interests and party political associations. (IV,iii,20)

Despite his conviction that morals is a deductive system, Locke never produced a definitive explanation of how the science of morality was possible. Instead, what we find are scattered comments, which do not add up to an a priori moral system. However, in Locke's view, morality is a science of great importance. Furthermore, it has important connections to his political philosophy, which is perhaps the most influential political theory of all time. For these reasons, we shall examine Locke's moral theory in this chapter under the cautionary proviso that Locke never produced a single work which reflects his mature views on morality. His moral thought must be collected from various sources and put together using intelligent supposition.

Three characterizations of Morality

Locke gives us three different schematic characterizations of morality. It is difficult to know for sure whether these represent different phases in his thought, or whether he thought all three characterizations amount in the final analysis to the same thing. The latter is more likely.

1) Natural Law

In the *Essay* Locke writes:

> Moral good or evil is only conformity or disagreement of our
> voluntary actions to some law (II, xxviii,5).

Locke claims that a law holds for all human beings independently of
all institutions. Such laws are knowable by reason. This is why
sometimes Locke's ethics is called rationalism.

For us today, Locke's terminology is a little confusing; he usually
calls these laws, the laws of nature or the natural law. Such phrases
refer to the basic rules which govern the behavior of the universe, such
as 'Everything must have a cause', but they also include the moral rules
to which all rational beings should conform their actions.

Locke takes his version of the natural law theory to contradict the
idea of innate moral knowledge. This makes his view different from the
traditional natural law theories that assert that conscience is innate
knowledge of moral principles. In opposition to this, Locke argues that
conscience is the opinion of the rightness or wrongness of one's own
actions, and such opinions may be derived from education or custom
(I,iii,8).

Locke's attack, however, is not directed against the truth of
fundamental moral principles. His main concern is that the innateness
hypothesis would deny the role of reason in morality. Of any practical
principle, we can ask what is the reason for it? This would not be so if
principles were innate. Locke's view is that God intended us to think
for ourselves (I,iv,12). For this reason, He gave us innate capacities,
and not innate ideas and knowledge. According to Locke, the claim that
a principle or piece of knowledge is innate is equivalent to the
affirmation that it does not need support from reason or experience.
This is what motivates his arguments against innateness.

Locke distinguishes three sorts of moral rules: the divine, the
civil, and the law of opinion. He says that, in accordance with the first,
people:

> Judge whether their actions are sins or duties; by the second,
> whether they be criminal or innocent; and by the third, whether
> they be virtues or vices. (II, xxviii,7)

Of these three, only the first defines the nature of moral obligation, and
it is to that we now turn.

2) God's Will

According to Locke, God's will is the true ground of morality. (I,iii,6) Being moral consists in following God's law. Locke argues that the concept of obligation requires the idea of law, which in turn requires the idea of a lawmaker. (I, iv, 8)

Since we may know God's will through revelation, Locke thinks that the Bible is a very important source for learning the nature of the moral law. However, as we warned in the previous chapter, although revelation can transcend reason, it cannot contradict it. Thus, relying on the Bible as a source of our understanding of morality is not an excuse for ignoring reason.

According to Locke, morality consists of laws. Laws are rules that are commanded by a someone who has the power to enforce them with punishment. For this reason, the idea of moral obligation requires the existence of God who commands such laws. Also, morality requires the concepts of punishment and reward for obeying and contravening the law. In this way, morality involves the idea of an after-life.

3) Pleasure

Locke claims that the good is whatever produces pleasure. He does not argue that the two terms 'good' and 'pleasant' are synonymous, but affirms that goodness can only be understood in terms of pleasure and badness, pain.

> That we call good which is apt to cause or increase pleasure, or diminish pain in us; or else to procure or preserve us the possession of any other good or absence of any other evil.
> (II,xx,2)

Locke obviously intends the word 'pleasure' to be taken broadly. He says that it may be called alternatively: happiness, satisfaction, delight (II,vii,2). It would include pleasures of the mind and of the body. 'Pleasure' for Locke, is a shorthand means to refer to what a person desires or prefers. Locke affirms that people desire very different things (II,xxi,55). As a consequence, Locke denies the usefulness of the ancient question: What way of living is the good life for a human being?

Locke holds that doing harm to a community is worse than doing a harm against an individual (King, ii, 95). On the basis of this, we may suppose that Locke would have claimed that an act which promotes more happiness for more people would be better than one which secures less happiness for fewer people. If so, his view would be a forerunner of Utilitarianism.

A major part of Locke's motivation for explaining moral beliefs in terms of pleasure and pain is to show how moral ideas fit into his overall empiricist framework. The concepts of good and bad are derived from our ideas of pleasure and pain. In other words, we do not need to postulate a different or special faculty to explain the origin of moral concepts. They are acquired from experience as are all other ideas.

Furthermore, Locke embraces a hedonist view of human motivation, according to which all our actions are motivated ultimately by the prospect of pleasure and the avoidance of pain. (II, xxi, 41) This does not exclude the happiness of others being part of one's own happiness. In this way, it is not necessarily an egoistic view. However, given such a view, it is understandable why Locke thinks that we can only make sense of the concepts of goodness and badness in terms of pleasure and pain.

The Unity of the Three

We have briefly examined three characterizations of morality that are to be found in the works of Locke. How can Locke reconcile these three different views of morality? The following quote encapsulates his overarching idea:

> What duty is cannot be understood without a law; nor a law be known or supposed without a law-maker, or without reward and punishment. (I,iii,12)

a) The First and the Second

The claim that to be moral we must conform our actions to the laws of nature is reconcilable with the claim that morality is based on God's will on the assumption that the laws of nature themselves come from God. In this way, Locke reconciles reason and religion. Reason tells us that we should follow the natural law. However, those same laws are divinely commanded. Consequently, the dictates of reason and the natural law will not conflict with the commands of God.

Because of this, the laws that we should obey because they are God's will are also the laws which reason would recommend to us. God wills what is rational. God does not will arbitrarily and therefore He chooses to command acts that are rational.

b) The Third

Locke distinguishes natural and moral good and bad. Natural good and bad arise from our natural inclinations, such as hunger. Locke says:

> naturally good and evil (is that) which, by the natural efficiency of things produces pleasure and pain in us (King, ii, 128).

On the other hand, something which is morally good produces a pleasure that is a reward from God. According to Locke, God attaches pleasure to certain kinds of acts, in order to reward us for obeying His laws. Locke writes:

> That is morally good which by the intervention of the will of an intelligent free agent, draws pleasure and pain after it, not by any natural consequence but by the intervention of that power. (King, ii, 128)

Given this distinction, the third characterization of morality can be reconciled with the second and the first. We can suppose that Locke's underlying idea is as follows: Through reason we can learn what God wills, for what God wills conforms to the laws of nature or the moral law. This is the rational ground of morality. What we might call the motivational ground of morality is pleasure.

As we saw earlier, Locke claims that people are motivated by pleasure. He also thinks that people can be weak-willed. Even people who believe in everlasting Hell still commit sins. Their wills are not determined by their beliefs about which actions would maximize happiness for them. They act against their own better judgment. For this reason, God must back up his laws with sanctions and rewards, or pain and pleasure.

In summary, Locke's idea of morality is that an act is morally good if it complies with a law which is given by God, and which God enforces with reward and punishment, through pleasure and pain. (II,xxviii, 5).

Although Locke thinks that knowledge of right and wrong can be derived by reasoning, he also thinks that revealed scripture is an important source of our understanding of morality. He claims that God created all persons free and equal. Consequently, the laws of nature affirm the natural equality of all persons, and on the basis of this, we have certain natural rights, including the right to freedom and ownership. These in turn are vital elements in Locke's political theory.

10
Politics:
Property and Power

"It is lawful for the people...to resist their King." (T.II.xix.232) These were revolutionary words in the turbulent England of the seventeenth century. They were also extraordinarily apt, as we shall see.

The Revolutionary Context

In 1679, less than twenty years after the restoration of Charles II, the political situation in England was threatening to become unstable again, despite the earlier yearnings for peace after the Civil War. The king of England is the head of the Anglican church. The legitimate heir to the throne was James, the younger brother of the king, Charles II. James was a Catholic. There were strong fears that he would try to impose his religion on the country. For this reason, Shaftesbury supported the succession of the illegitimate but Protestant son of Charles II, the Duke of Monmouth. Shaftesbury organized clubs in support of Monmouth and tried to rouse opposition to the succession of James. As a consequence, Shaftesbury was arrested and sent to the Tower of London in 1681 on a charge of treason and Locke fled to Holland.

In 1685 James become king. Soon after, the illegitimate claimant to the throne, Monmouth, launched a rebellion that failed and he was executed. These events seem to have hardened James II, who appointed

Roman Catholics to key positions throughout England, ignoring existing laws favoring the Anglican religion of the country. Late that year he disbanded Parliament. He issued a Declaration of Indulgence invoking the power to dispense with existing laws to ensure freedom of religion. There was a huge groundswell of popular opinion against the king. People began to fear that James would impose a Catholic despotism, similar to that of Louis XIV in France. When France threatened war against Holland, this fear took on a new urgency. Despite the fact that his daughter Mary was married to the Dutch regent, William of Orange, it became unclear which side James would support in conflict between Protestant Holland and Catholic France. In April 1688 William of Orange decided that, if invited by the English, he would try to usurp the throne of James. He began to prepare to invade Britain.

Events became more dramatic when James had a son in June 1688. Now there was a clear legitimate heir to the throne and something for the Catholics to fight for. That same month, James realized that his son-in-law and daughter were preparing to take the throne from him. He also realized that his own actions had been very unpopular, and so he began to back-pedal. In September, he issued a proclamation promising to uphold the laws of the land and summon parliament. He assured the Dutch that he had no secret treaty with France. He reversed some of his earlier decisions. But it was already too late. At the beginning of November, Prince William and his army landed at Torbay in the west of England.

The English people welcomed the Protestant prince and the king's daughter. Towns surrendered without a shot. James' other daughter, Princess Anne, joined the side of her sister, as did many of the Tory families who normally supported royal causes. James had no real support. He fled to France and William of Orange entered London.

A special session of Parliament was called for January 1689 to decide the future government of the country. The House of Commons was about two-thirds Whigs, in support of the Protestant prince. However, the House of Lords had a majority of Tories. The scene was set for a dramatic debate.

The Commons put forward two resolutions. First, that James had "endeavored to subvert the constitution by breaking the original contract between king and people" and that in so doing he had effectively abdicated his throne. Second, that it was "inconsistent with the safety and welfare" of Protestant England to be governed by a Catholic king. The House of Lords accepted the second motion, but not the first. The first motion suggested that a king could be voted out of office for failure to perform his duty and thereby violated the principle of hereditary rights. The Tories would not agree to that.

Deadlock was broken when the princess Mary, James' eldest daughter, declared that she and her husband would rule jointly. The Lords agreed to the idea that James had abdicated by fleeing the country and William and Mary were proclaimed king and queen in February 1689.

These dramatic events ignited powerful political debates. Locke's greatest political work, the *Two Treatises on Government,* primarily justifies the right to resist an unjust authority. It is a justification of revolution against absolute monarchy. Consequently, its publication in August 1689 was very apt. In fact, Locke had written the majority of the manuscript before he left for Holland in 1683, at the time when he was serving Shaftesbury, during the earlier controversy about James' ascension to the throne.

After his return to England in early 1689, Locke worked furiously on his old manuscript, updating it so that it would support the "throne of our great restorer, our present King William." Locke's justification involves a clear articulation and defense of the principles that government must be by consent of those governed and that a ruler without the confidence of the people has no right to govern.

Locke's theory consists of five elements:

1) The criticism of the idea that kings have a divine right to rule
2) The theory of consent that gives governments' their legitimacy.
3) The theory of trust which interprets the relation between the Government and the people.
4) The theory of property: how people acquire the right to own private property
5) The practice or application of the above within the context of Britain of the time

Against the Divine Right of Kings

Locke wrote his book in part to refute the theories of Sir Robert Filmer who favored the divine right of kings to rule over their subjects. Filmer wrote his book, *A Defense of the Natural Power of Kings against the Unnatural Liberty of the People,* around 1640, and it became influential during the reign of Charles II as a clear and forceful articulation of the Royalist position. Naturally, it also became important for the Whigs, as the definitive book to refute, especially when they were trying to argue for the exclusion of James II.

The starting point of Filmer's theory is that it is wrong to commit suicide. According to Filmer, the prohibition of suicide shows that a person is not the owner of his or her own life. Only God is. This demonstrates that rulers cannot derive their right to rule from the people themselves, but only from God, since God is the owner of all.

Furthermore, when a subject threatens the public good, a ruler does have the right to take away that person's life. This fact is only compatible with the Christian prohibition of suicide given that rulers derive their right directly from God. By trying to show that they do, Filmer argues for the divine right of kings. The right to rule is a gift from God.

Filmer backs this argument with a historical explanation. According to the Old Testament, God gave the Earth to Adam. He gave Adam the right to ownership and all the political authority derived from that. Adam's original right has subsequently been subdivided and passed on as an inheritance to political rulers or kings. This political authority remains an expression of God's will. God, who is the owner of everything, appoints certain people to rule over parts of His Creation, on His behalf. Hence, the divine right of kings.

This theory denies the idea that rulers rule by the consent of the people. Therefore, it also denies the claim that the people have a right to rebel against their ruler, when he or she threatens the public good. Therefore, Filmer's theory would make it impossible to justify the act of Parliament in 1689 that replaced James II with William and Mary.

In reply to Filmer, Locke distinguishes the right to rule and the obligation to obey. For the most part, citizens have the obligation to obey the ruler for the sake of peace and order, which are necessary for a good life. However, rulers have the right to rule only when their commands deserve respect and obedience. When those commands threaten peace and order, the subjects have the right to resist. In other words, for Locke, political authority is not based on a property right inherited from God, but is based on the need for order and peace.

According to Locke, the Christian prohibition of suicide does not show that God has given rulers property rights over the people. Instead, it shows that killing is wrong because of the laws that God has set for human life. The Christian prohibition demonstrates the great value of human life. In contrast, Filmer's position denies this value by implying that all people are the slaves or property of their ruler. According to Locke, this contravenes what God has ordained.

Consent

Locke says that to elucidate the basis of political power, we must explain how people left the original, non-political state of nature and, by entering into a social contract, formed a civil society governed by laws.

77

a) <u>The state of nature</u>: By nature all people are "equal and independent." (T. II, 6) According to Locke, in the state of nature, prior to the formation of any civil society, people would act according to their desires, but as constrained by their reason. Insofar as they are rational, people would make their actions conform to the moral laws of nature, as known through reason. On the whole, in a state of nature, people would not kill each other, break promises, and use others. In other words, according to Locke, in the state of nature people would not be completely amoral. They would still be under an obligation to follow the moral law. However, they would be free from social constraints and actually would obey the moral laws of nature only insofar as they happen to be rational. Furthermore, people are often irrational. Consequently, in a state of nature, people easily may enter into a state of war, in which they use force to seize the property of others or protect themselves from such incursions. In other words, the state of nature can be peaceful, but it is unstable, and may degenerate easily into a state of war. For this reason, it is uncertain. According to Locke, to overcome this uncertainty, people form a civil society.

Furthermore, Locke says that the state of nature lacks:

> An established, settled, known law, received and allowed by common consent to be the standard of right and wrong and the common measure to decide all controversies between them.

In affirming this Locke is not claiming that morality is determined by such a social law. Right and wrong do not depend on common consent, but rather on the law of nature, as we saw in the previous chapter. Nevertheless, common agreement is needed for people to live together in a more secure environment. It is necessary, not for the definition of right and wrong or morality, but rather for its execution or practice. In the state of nature, people have no way to settle disagreements about the law of nature and each may punish the other according to his judgment of what the law of nature dictates. This is a source of insecurity. In contrast, to live securely, people need openly stated and commonly known expectations of each other. Therefore, we need laws enforced by a political power.

Furthermore, as we shall see later, we also need such laws for the sake of our prosperity, so that we can own more property. This is because property rights can be upheld with security and peace only with public and enforceable laws.

b) <u>The social contract</u>: By giving up political power, the individual gains security and the possibility of owning more property. Locke defines political power as:

> a right of making laws with the penalties of death and consequently all the less penalties, for the regulating and preserving of property, of employing the force of the community in the execution of such laws and in the defense of the commonwealth from foreign injury and all this only for the public good (T. II,3)

In other words, to gain security for themselves and their property, individuals make an agreement to form a society according to which they give up their right to enforce morality to a government.

Each individual enters into such a contract on his or her own behalf. The agreement of past generations cannot bind the present generation. This social contract is made by tacit agreement. One agrees to it by remaining part of the community when one becomes an adult. The only way to dissent is to depart.

This analysis of the origin of society shows the purpose of government. It is for the mutual preservation of life, liberty and property. (T. II, 125) From this it follows that government should not control and rule. It should serve. According to Locke, government is not a matter of subjugation, but of contract. It also follows that the individual should give up his or her rights to the minimum degree necessary for the mutual protection of the members of society. The individual should not give up more than he or she needs to.

Trust

For Locke, the social contract consists of trust. Trust binds together a society. According to Locke, we are under a moral obligation to trust each other. It is a duty according to the law of nature, which reflects our dependence on God. Locke's idea is that God intended humans to live together in communities, but the more we ignore our dependence on God, the more we tend to live as isolated and distrustful individuals. So, according to Locke, we have a moral obligation to trust each other, and to live up to that trust. To fail in either duty is to help society disintegrate.

For the sake of peace and prosperity, people need to trust each other and even more so, their government or rulers. However, this does not mean those rulers will actually live up to that trust. According to

Locke, part of the function of a ruler is to provide impartial judgement. This is the main reason for the social contract; individuals give up political power to a government, so that there is a central authority who establishes and enforces a common known law for the stability of society, which permits the development of property. Consequently, rulers deserve the trust and obedience of their subjects only insofar as they administer the law impartially.

A ruler who does not do this is a tyrant. Locke gives two definitions of tyranny. First, a tyrant uses his political power for his own benefit rather than for the good of the public (T. II, xviii, 200). Second, Locke defines a tyranny as "the use of force without authority" (T. II,xiii,155). In other words, a ruler who uses force beyond what the law allows becomes a tyrrant. These two characterization of tyranny depend respectively on two general features of politics. The first characterization depends on the end or purpose of government, and the second on the origin of political power.

In making these points, Locke claims that no person is beyond the law (T. II,vii, 94). Everyone is subject to the laws of the land, including a king. In this way, Locke explicitly draws a distinction between a law and the will of a ruler.

When a tyrant acts against the law or outside of the law to hurt people, then he has set himself into a state of war with those people. He has become an unjust aggressor. This is effectively the same as declaring war on those individuals, who consequently have the right to defend themselves.

Property Rights

To answer Filmer, Locke also has to explain how individual property rights can be justified. The problem he must address is how to reconcile the claim that God gave the Earth to humans collectively with the affirmation of private property rights. Filmer argues that such a reconciliation is impossible, and he uses this point to argue that God bestows the Earth to divinely appointed rulers, the political descents of Adam, rather than to humanity as a whole. To counter Filmer's argument, Locke must answer the question: How can the idea of humanity as a whole receiving God's gift be compatible with individual private property?

The essence of Locke's brilliantly simple answer is labor. Labor belongs to the person who works. By applying labor to raw materials and other unowned things, a person can make those things his or her private property. That is the person acquires private property rights over land, minerals and energy through his or her work.

In this way, Locke can resolve the conflict between the idea of God bestowing the planet to humanity generally and the concept of private property. He can also answer Filmer who thinks that such rights derive from God, but via a king or ruler. Locke thinks they derive from God via the labor of the individual person.

Locke supposes that everyone is born with God-given rights. Of these a primary one is the right to freedom of action, without being subject to the will of another, so long as one conforms to the laws of morality. Locke thinks that, because we are equally members of the same species, all people are equal in this right. In this sense, God created us free and equal, and because of this, we are under an obligation not to harm others and to promote the "preservation of all mankind." Consequently, in this way the rich and poor are equal and wealth does not convey the right to greater political power. This right to freedom of action is the basis of the claim that each person has a right to their own labor.

These assertions illustrate that, according to Locke, morality is defined primarily by the Law of Nature, as laid down by God. People have rights and obligations in the state of nature, prior to the formation of any society. The right to property does not arise out of the social contract. Rather it arises from the right to our own labor and from the right to act freely, within the moral law.

Despite this, the right to property has important political implications. According to Locke, the politics of a society should based on the principles of natural morality. He says:

> The municipal laws of countries are only so far right as they are founded on the Law of Nature by which they are to be regulated and interpreted (T. II,ii,9)

As a consequence of this, Locke claims that a monarch cannot legitimately levy taxes on his own authority. He requires the consent of the people or of their legislative representatives in order to not "invade the fundamental law of property" (T. II, xi,139). He says:

> The supreme power cannot take from any man any part of his property without his own consent (T. II,xi,138)

However, according to Locke, the moral basis of politics also places limits on the right to own property. Property rights are not absolute. They are limited by other moral obligations. In particular, we have an obligation not to waste. The ownership rights are derived from

God, and so we have a duty to be good stewards or guardians of our possessions.

Furthermore, according to Locke, every individual has a natural right to subsistence. As we have seen, Locke thinks that we have a moral obligation to promote the common or general good. This reflects the right of each person to what they need to subsist. As a consequence of this moral right, one may have an obligation to others which overrides one's own property rights. For example, suppose that I buy some goods from a very poor man, knowing that if I insist on paying the minimum market price, he will starve. In such case, Locke would claim that I have done something morally wrong. His need generates a moral right which overrides my property rights. Locke thinks that this moral right also has political implications. Governments have an obligation to provide relief for the poor.

How does Locke reconcile the private right to property and the interests of the community or the general good? In part, by describing a process by which property becomes more and more socially institutionalized. First, in the state of nature, when people live as hunter gatherers, property is defined by a person's natural right to free action and hence right over his or her own labor. It is also defined by the right to use natural resources to provide for one's own subsistence and needs.

Second, as agriculture becomes more settled and cities develop, individuals in communities agree to use money. They agree to accept money in exchange for the goods produced by their labor. In so doing, they permit persons to own beyond what they need for their consumption needs, because this is what the use of money makes possible. However, the use of money also makes it possible for more people to become better off; it increases "the common stock of mankind" (T. II,v, 37). For this reason, the invention of money is in accord with the moral law. However, this economic development necessitates the existence of contracts and property laws to regulate commerce. Property titles and contracts are needed to prevent quarrels, and laws-courts are necessary to resolve them.

Laws to regulate property require the existence of some form of government. In the early stages of society, the laws needed were few and correspondingly the most appropriate form of government was also simple: monarchy. Locke claims that, as a society grows wealthy and becomes more industrialized and commercial, its laws become more complex. This requires a more complex form of government described by Locke's theory of the social contract. As the wealth of society increases, leaders are more likely to act in their own self-interest, and so we need to balance the power of government, "by placing several parts of it in different hands" (T.II.viii.111).

In effect, Locke's account of the origin and development of property provides an explanation of the social contract and thus a moral justification for constitutional government.

Practice

In summary, as well rejecting the arguments of Filmer for the divine right of kings, Locke expounds a comprehensive political theory. He argues that the aim of government should be the common good of the people and that the source of political power is the consent of the people. He tries to establish the moral and political basis of individual property rights. He argues that all people should be equal before the law. In doing all of this, Locke constructs a political theory that allows him to distinguish between a legitimate ruler and a tyrant.

Now we should see how Locke applies these aspects of his theory to the political situation of England of the time. In particular, how does Locke's theory justify Parliament's overthrowing of James II and replacing him with William and Mary?

First, the background. Locke feels that the best form of Government should include elements from the three types of Government, monarchy, oligarchy and democracy. He is in favor of an elected legislative assembly with the power to "direct how the force of the commonwealth shall be employed for preserving the community and the members of it." (T. II,143). This legislative or law-making body is made up of representatives elected by the people.

Locke distinguishes this legislative branch from the executive which puts the laws into practice, and from the federative which is concerned with foreign affairs. He thinks that the executive and federative functions can be combined in one person, the monarch. Although Locke does separate these political functions, he does not distinguish the executive and judiciary, as we do today.

In short, the monarch is responsible to the legislative assembly, which in turn is responsible to the people. In this sense the people have supreme power in Locke's theory (T. II, 149). However, once the representatives are elected and the assembly is in session, it is supreme. However, the assembly gives discretion to the executive to act in the public good. The legislature delegates to the king.

The upshot is that the community has the supreme authority. The community passes political power to the legislative assembly who in turn delegate authority to the executive. As a consequence, the people has the right to depose any executive who tries to become a tyrant or gain absolute power for him or herself.

What actions would constitute a king's becoming a tyrant in the context of the political situation of Britain of the 17th century? Any action that constitutes a "breach of trust" and an attempt "to subvert the Government" would be an act of tyranny. First, in 17th century England, the king had the power to call or dissolve Parliament. However, according to Locke, this power is based on a trust placed by people in the elected Parliament which in turn places trust in the executive or monarch. A king's persistent refusal to summon the legislature would amount to an abuse of this discretionary power and an attempt to undermine the political system by changing the balance of power. Furthermore, it would deprive the people of their right to have elected representatives. For these reasons, it would count as an act of tyranny. In fact, between 1681 and 1685 the king, Charles II, did not call the Parliament into session.

Second, a king might try to subvert the political power of the legislature in other ways, for example, by bribing or threatening the members of Parliament, or by trying to alter the ways elections are carried out. Third, he may try to deliver the country to a foreign power (T. II,xix, 219). Fourth, he may abandon his duty and fail to put the laws passed by the Parliament into practice. Each of these cases would constitute a breach of trust and hence, an act of tyranny that would warrant resisting the king.

Locke's theory had its greatest application on the so-called new continent. Locke wrote: "In the beginning all the world was America" (T. II,49). He may have understood that the new continent presented opportunities for his new political ideas. He helped draft the state constitution for Carolina. However, he could never have imagined that the USA would become an independent country with a constitution that owes much to his political philosophy. Much less could he have imagined that his revolutionary ideas would become orthodoxy.

BIBLIOGRAPHY

Aaron, R.J. *John Locke*, Oxford, 1971

Ayers, M., *Locke* (2 Vols), Routledge, 1991

Chappell, V., *The Cambridge Companion to Locke*, Cambridge, 1994

Colman, J., *Locke's Moral Philosophy,* Edinburgh, 1983

Cranston, M, *John Locke: a Biography,* London, 1957

Dunn, J., *Locke*, Oxford, 1984

Hutchinson, R., *Locke in France 1688-1734*, Oxford, 1991

Jolley, N., *Leibniz and Locke*, Oxford, 1984

Jolley, N., *Locke: His Philosophical Thought*, Oxford, 1999

King, Peter, ed.,*The Life and Letters of John Locke,* 2 vols.

Locke, John, *An Essay Concerning Human Understanding,* ed. P. Nidditch, Oxford, 1978

Locke, John, *Two Treatises of Government*, ed. P. Laslett, Cambridge, 1987

Locke, John, *A Letter Concerning Toleration,* ed.J.Tully, Indianapolis, 1983

Locke, John, *Essays on the Law of Nature,* ed. W.von Leyden, Oxford, 1954

Locke, John, *The Correspondence of John Locke,* ed. E. de Beer, Oxford, 1976-89

Locke, John, *The Works of John Locke,* 10 vols., Aalen, 1963

Mackie, John, *Problems from Locke,* Oxford, 1976

O'Connor, D.J., *John Locke,* London, 1952

Rogers, G.A. , *Locke's Enlightenment,* Georg Olms Verlag, 1998

Rogers, G.A. , *Locke's Philosophy: Content and Context,* Oxford, 1994

Schouls, P, *Reasoned Freedom: John Locke and the Enlightenment,* Ithica, N.Y., 1992

Spellman, W., *John Locke and the Problem of Depravity,* Oxford, 1988

Thomson, G., *Descartes to Kant,* Waveland Press, 1998

Tipton, I.C. (ed.), *Locke on Human Understanding,* Oxford, 1977

Woolhouse, R.S., *Locke's Philosophy of Science and Knowledge,* Oxford, 1971

Woolhouse, R.S., *Locke,* Brighton, 1983

Yolton, J., *Locke; an Introduction,* Oxford, 1985